THE REVELS PLAYS

Former general editors
David Bevington
F. David Hoeniger
E. A. J. Honigmann
Clifford Leech
J. R. Mulryne
Eugene M. Waith
Martin White

General editors
Karen Britland, Richard Dutton, Alison Findlay,
Rory Loughnane, Helen Ostovich and Barbara Ravelhofer

DICK OF DEVONSHIRE

Manchester University Press

THE REVELS PLAYS

To buy or to find out more about the books currently available in this series, please go to: https://manchesteruniversitypress.co.uk/series/revels-plays/

THE REVELS PLAYS

DICK OF DEVONSHIRE

BY THOMAS HEYWOOD

edited by Kate Ellis

MANCHESTER
UNIVERSITY PRESS

Introduction, critical apparatus, etc.
© Kate Ellis 2024

The right of Kate Ellis to be identified as the editor of this work
has been asserted by them in accordance with the Copyright,
Designs and Patents Act 1988.

This edition published by Manchester University Press
Oxford Road, Manchester M13 9PL

www.manchesteruniversitypress.co.uk

British Library Cataloguing-in-Publication Data
A catalogue record for this book is available from the
British Library

ISBN   978 0 7190 9936 6   hardback

First published 2024

The publisher has no responsibility for the persistence or accuracy
of URLs for any external or third-party internet websites referred
to in this book, and does not guarantee that any content on such
websites is, or will remain, accurate or appropriate.

Typeset
by New Best-set Typesetters Ltd

Contents

ILLUSTRATIONS	vi
GENERAL EDITORS' PREFACE	vii
PREFACE	x
ABBREVIATIONS AND REFERENCES	xii
INTRODUCTION	I
The quest for authorship	I
Date and sources	3
The play	9
The text	13
Theatrical history	17
Stagecraft	19
The occasion of the play	24
Anglo-Spanish relations in the play	27
This edition	30
DICK OF DEVONSHIRE	35
APPENDICES	131
FURTHER READING	152
INDEX	154

Illustrations

1   Factor analysis of *Dick of Devonshire* and plays written
solely by Thomas Heywood   3

2   Title page woodcut of Richard Peeke's *Three to One*
© Huntington Library, San Marino, California   5

3   Drake's Island, Plymouth (formerly St Nicholas's
Island, the 'little island before Plymouth', 4.3.112)
© Amy Sampson Photography, 2015   28

General editors' preface

Clifford Leech conceived of the Revels Plays as a series in the mid-1950s, modelling the project on the New Arden Shakespeare. The aim, as he wrote in 1958, was 'to apply to Shakespeare's predecessors, contemporaries, and successors the methods that are now used in Shakespeare's editing'. The plays chosen were to include well-known works from the early Tudor period to about 1700, as well as others less familiar but of literary and theatrical merit. 'The plays included', Leech wrote, 'should be such as to deserve and indeed demand performance'. We owe it to Clifford Leech that the idea became reality. He set the high standards of the series, ensuring that editors of individual volumes produced work of lasting merit, equally useful for teachers and students, theatre directors and actors. Clifford Leech remained General Editor until 1971, and was succeeded by F. David Hoeniger, who retired in 1985.

Ever since then, the Revels Plays have been under the direction of four or five general editors: initially David Bevington, E. A. J. Honigmann, J. R. Mulryne, and E. M. Waith. E. A. J. Honigmann retired in 2000 and was succeeded by Richard Dutton. E. M. Waith retired in 2003 and was succeeded by Alison Findlay and Helen Ostovich. J. R. Mulryne retired in 2010. Published originally by Methuen, the series is now published by the Manchester University Press, embodying essentially the same format, scholarly character, and high editorial standards of the series as first conceived. The series now concentrates on plays from the period 1558–1642. Some slight changes have been made: for example, starting in 1996 each index lists proper names and topics in the introduction and commentary, whereas earlier indexes focused only on words and phrases for which the commentary provided a gloss. Notes to the introduction are now placed together at the end, not at the foot of, the page. Collation and commentary notes continue, however, to appear on the relevant pages.

The introduction to each Revels play undertakes to offer, among other matters, a critical appraisal of the play's significant themes and images, its poetic and verbal fascinations, its historical context, its characteristics as a piece for the theatre, and its uses of the stage for

GENERAL EDITORS' PREFACE

which it was designed. Stage history is an important part of the story. In addition, the introduction presents as lucidly as possible the criteria for choice of copy-text and the editorial methods employed in presenting the play to a modern reader. The introduction also considers the play's date and, where relevant, its sources, together with its place in the work of the author and in the theatre of its time. If the play is by an author not previously represented in the series, a brief biography is provided.

The text of each Revels play, in accordance with established practice in the series, is edited afresh from the original text of best authority (in a few instances, texts), in modern spelling and punctuation and with speech headings that are consistent throughout. Elisions in the original are also silently regularised, except where metre would be affected by the change. Emendations, as distinguished from modernized spellings and punctuation, are introduced only in instances where error is patent or at least very probable, and where the corrected reading is persuasive. Act divisions are given only if they appear in the original, or if the structure of the play clearly points to them. Those act and scene divisions not in the original are provided in small type. Square brackets are also used for any other additions to, or changes in, the stage directions of the original.

Rather than provide a comprehensive and historical variorum collation, Revels Plays editions focus on those variants which require the critical attention of serious textual students. All departures of substance from the copy-text are listed, including any significant relineation and those changes in punctuation which involve to any degree a decision between alternative interpretations. The collation notes do not include such accidentals as turned letters or changes in the font. Additions to stage directions are not noted in the collations, since those additions are already made clear by the use of brackets. On the other hand, press corrections in the copy-text are duly collated, as based on a careful consultation of as many copies of the original edition or editions as are needed to ensure that the printing history of those originals is accurately reported. Of later emendations of the text by subsequent editors, only those are reported which still deserve attention as alternative readings.

One of the hallmarks of the Revels Plays is the thoroughness of their annotations. Besides explaining the meanings of difficult words and passages, the annotations provide commentary on customs or usage, on the text, on stage business – indeed, on anything that can

GENERAL EDITORS' PREFACE ix

be pertinent and helpful. On occasion, when long notes are required and are too lengthy to fit comfortably at the foot of the page below the text, they are printed at the end of the complete text.

Appendices are used to present any commendatory poems on the dramatist and play in question, documents about the play's reception and contemporary history, classical sources, casting analyses, music, and any other relevant material.

Each volume contains an index to the commentary, in which particular attention is drawn to meanings for words not listed in the OED, and (starting in 1996, as indicated above) an indexing of proper names and topics in the introduction and commentary.

Our hope is that plays edited in this fashion will promote further scholarly and theatrical investigation of one of the richest periods in theatrical history.

KAREN BRITLAND
RICHARD DUTTON
ALISON FINDLAY
RORY LOUGHNANE
HELEN OSTOVICH
BARBARA RAVELHOFER

Preface

In 1625 Richard Peeke, a soldier from Tavistock in Devon, was captured by Spanish troops during the ill-fated Cadiz expedition. He was challenged to demonstrate his military prowess by fighting three Spanish soldiers. When Peeke defeated all three, armed only with a quarterstaff, the King of Spain declared him a hero and offered him honorary Spanish citizenship. He declined, swearing continued allegiance to the English crown, and returned home from Spain as a celebrated war hero. He was granted an audience with Charles I, wrote a flamboyant autobiographical account, and was immortalised a year later in this play, *Dick of Devonshire*. Yet despite the citation of his exploits on several martial arts websites, and amateur reconstructions of the combat being uploaded to social media, I am aware that many readers opening this book will be encountering Peeke's story for the first time. Because the play was not printed until the nineteenth century, and no record of a performance has been found, the dramatic manuscript gathered dust in the British Library until recent years, and yet the worst thing to do with a play that has faded from the national consciousness is nothing. The more *Dick of Devonshire* is brought out into the light, the more the play can contribute to current scholarly debate, inspire further research and generate ideas. The ability of such a play to contribute in this way is diminished greatly if it is left to languish in relative obscurity. Exciting research has been carried out on lost plays, by scholars such as Matthew Steggle, Roslyn Knutson, David McGinnis, and Lucy Munro, because of the contribution they believe these plays can make to critical discussion. *Dick of Devonshire* was never lost. It had just been forgotten, until now. If a lost play that survives only in fragmentary textual traces can make such a contribution, so too can this play, a play that exists in manuscript in its entirety.

This edition would not have been possible without help from many people. Above all, I am grateful to Tracey Hill and Ian Gadd of Bath Spa University, for their unending enthusiasm, support, and guidance. They have been a constant source of inspiration, challenge, and encouragement for many years. A significant debt of gratitude is also due to Matthew Steggle, Alan Marshall, Joanne

PREFACE xi

Wrigley, Heather Froelich, Carole Sutton, and Roberta Anderson. Particular thanks are also due to Manchester University Press, to Richard Dutton, David Bevington, and Matthew Frost, for their expertise, time, and patience. I could not have conducted my research without the expert help of the library staff of the British Library, the Huntington Library, California, Bath Spa University, the University of Exeter, the University of Plymouth, and Downside Abbey. Some sections of the introductory notes were given as conference papers; I am grateful to the organisers of those conferences, and to the delegates who shared their insights with me, most notably Barbara Ravelhofer, Richard Rowland, and Julie Sanders. Thank you to the members of the former Playwrights' Forum at the Theatre Royal Plymouth, particularly David Prescott, for their interest in the project and their lively debates about the play's possible authorship. Special thanks to Rachel Hogden. As always, all my love and thanks to my family: to Mum, Dad, Claire, Leigh, Henry, Thomas, and Nancy.

Abbreviations and references

MSS AND EDITIONS

Bullen
A. H. Bullen, ed., *A Collection of Old English Plays*, vol. 2 (London: Wyman & Sons, 1882)

Malone
Anon., *Dick of Devonshire*, ed. James G. McManaway and Mary R. McManaway (Oxford: Malone Society Reprints, 1955)

Q
British Library MS Egerton 1994, fols. 30–51, Anon., *Dick of Devonshire*

OTHER PRIMARY TEXTS

Cecil
Edward Cecil, *A Journall, and Relation of the Action Which by His Majesties Commandement, Edward Lord Cecil, Baron of Putney, and Vicount of Wimbledon, Admirall, and Lieutenant Generall of His Majesties Forces, Did Undertake Upon the Coast of Spaine* (London: Elliot's Court Press, 1626)

Game at Chess
Thomas Middleton, *A Game at Chess*, ed. T. H. Howard-Hill (Manchester: Manchester University Press, 1993)

Greg
W. W. Greg, *Dramatic Documents from the Elizabethan Playhouse: Stage Plots: Actors' Parts: Prompt Books*, 2 vols (Oxford: Clarendon Press, 1931)

Grosart
Alexander B. Grosart, ed., *The Voyage to Cadiz in 1625. Being a Journal Written by John Glanville, Secretary to the Lord Admiral of the Fleet (Sir E. Cecil)* (London: Camden Society, 1883)

Peeke
Richard Peeke, *Three to One: Being, an English-Spanish Combat, Performed by a Westerne Gentleman, of Tavystoke in Devon Shire with an English Quarter-Staffe, against Three Spanish Rapiers and Poniards* (London: Augustine Mathewes for John Trundle, 1626)

xii

ABBREVIATIONS AND REFERENCES xiii

Shakespeare	William Shakespeare, *The RSC Shakespeare: The Complete Works*, ed. Jonathan Bate and Eric Rasmussen (Basingstoke: Palgrave Macmillan, 2007)

OTHER WORKS

Bedford et al	Ronald Bedford, Lloyd Davis, and Philippa Kelly, *Early Modern English Lives: Autobiography and Self-Representation, 1500–1660* (Aldershot: Ashgate, 2007)
Beeson	Mark Beeson, *A History of Dartmoor Theatre Part One: 1325–1660* (Exeter: Devonshire Association, 1998)
Bentley	G. E. Bentley, *The Jacobean and Caroline Stage*, 7 vols (Oxford: Clarendon Press, 1941)
Birch	Thomas Birch, ed., *The Court and Times of Charles I*, vol. 1 (London: Henry Colburn, 1848)
Boas	F. S. Boas, *Thomas Heywood* (London: Williams & Norgate, 1950)
Boswell	Eleanore Boswell, 'Young Mr Cartwright', *The Modern Language Review*, 24.2 (1929), 125–42
Clare	Janet Clare, *Art Made Tongue-Tied by Authority: Elizabethan and Jacobean Dramatic Censorship*, 2nd edn (Manchester: Manchester University Press, 1999)
Clark	A. M. Clark, 'A Bibliography of Thomas Heywood', *Oxford Bibliographical Society, Proceedings and Papers* (1922–26), i
Collier	J. Payne Collier, ed., *Trevelyan Papers, 3 parts* (London: Camden Society, 1857–72)
Craig	Hugh Craig, 'Style, Statistics, and New Models of Authorship', *Early Modern Literary Studies*, 15.1 (2009–10), 1–42
Dessen and Thomson	Alan C. Dessen and Leslie Thomson, *A Dictionary of Stage Directions in English Drama, 1580–1642* (Cambridge: Cambridge University Press, 2000)
Dustagheer	Sarah Dustagheer, 'Appendix: List of Plays Performed at Indoor Playhouses, 1575–1642',

xiv ABBREVIATIONS AND REFERENCES

	in *Moving Shakespeare Indoors: Performance and Repertoire in the Jacobean Playhouse*, ed. Andrew Gurr and Farah Karim-Cooper (Cambridge: Cambridge University Press, 2014), 252–9
Fleay	F. J. Fleay, *A Biographical Chronicle of the English Drama, 1559–1642* (1891)
Frey and Lieblein	Christopher Frey and Leanore Lieblein, '"My breasts sear'd": The Self-Starved Female Body and "A Woman Killed with Kindness"', *Early Theatre*, 7.1 (2004), 45–66
Greatley-Hirsch et al	Brett Greatley-Hirsch, Matteo Pangallo, and Rachel White, '"Text up his name": The Authorship of the Manuscript Play *Dick of Devonshire*', forthcoming in *Studies in Philology*, 121.1 (2024)
Hammer	Paul E. J. Hammer, 'Myth-Making: Politics, Propaganda and the Capture of Cadiz in 1596', *The Historical Journal*, 40 (1997), 621–42
Hoenselaars	A. J. Hoenselaars, *Images of Englishmen and Foreigners in the Drama of Shakespeare and his Contemporaries: A Study of Stage Characters and National Identity in English Renaissance Drama, 1558–1642* (Madison, NJ: Fairleigh Dickinson University Presses, 1992)
Howard-Hill	T. H. Howard-Hill, *Middleton's 'Vulgar Pasquin': Essays on a 'Game at Chess'* (Newark, DE: Associated University Presses, 1995)
Ioppolo	Grace Ioppolo, 'Thomas Heywood, Just in Time', *Early Theatre*, 17.2 (2014), 122–32
Long	William B. Long, 'Playhouse Shadows: The Manuscript Behind *Dick of Devonshire*', *Early Theatre*, 17.2 (2014), 146–68
Lopez	Jeremy Lopez, *Constructing the Early Modern Canon* (Cambridge: Cambridge University Press, 2014)
Manning	R. B. Manning, *An Apprenticeship in Arms: The Origins of the British Army, 1585–1702* (Oxford: Oxford University Press, 2006)
Marchitello	Howard Marchitello, '(Dis)embodied Letters and *The Merchant of Venice*: Writing, Editing,

ABBREVIATIONS AND REFERENCES xv

	History', *English Literary History*, 62 (1995), 237–65
McManaway	James G. McManaway, 'Latin Title-Page Mottoes as a Clue to Dramatic Authorship', *The Library*, 26 (1995)
Munro	Lucy Munro, 'Music and Sound', in *The Oxford Handbook of Early Modern Theatre*, ed. Richard Dutton (2011; online edn, Oxford Academic, 18 September 2012), https://doi.org/10.1093/oxfordhb/9780199697861.001.0001
ODNB	*Oxford Dictionary of National Biography*
OED	*Oxford English Dictionary*
Palfrey and Stern	Simon Palfrey and Tiffany Stern, *Shakespeare in Parts* (Oxford: Oxford University Press, 2007)
Peters	Julie Stone Peters, *Theatre of the Book 1480–1880: Print, Text and Performance in Europe* (Oxford: Oxford University Press, 2000)
Rowland	Richard Rowland, *Thomas Heywood's Theatre, 1599–1639* (Farnham: Ashgate, 2010)
Stern	Tiffany Stern, *Documents of Performance in Early Modern England* (Cambridge: Cambridge University Press, 2009)
Stewart	Alan Stewart, *Shakespeare's Letters* (Oxford: Oxford University Press, 2008)
Taylor	Gary Taylor, 'Thomas Middleton, Thomas Dekker, and "The Bloody Banquet"', *The Papers of the Bibliographical Society of America*, 94.2 (2000), 197–233
Taylor and Lavagnino	Gary Taylor and John Lavagnino, eds., *Thomas Middleton and Early Modern Textual Culture: A Companion to the Collected Works* (Oxford: Oxford University Press, 2007)

Introduction

THE QUEST FOR AUTHORSHIP

Dick of Devonshire has been traditionally cited as an anonymous play, the identity of the author lost. The title page of MS Egerton 1994 does not include an authorial credit and the manuscript itself was prepared by a scribe, so the handwriting cannot be compared to contemporary autographs.

Thomas Heywood has long been the primary authorial candidate, proposed first by A. H. Bullen, tentatively, in his 1882 edition of the play:

> As to the authorship of the play, though I should be loath to speak with positiveness, I feel bound to put forward a claim for Thomas Heywood ... Now, when we open *Dick of Devonshire*, the naturalness and simplicity of the first scene at once suggest Heywood's hand. In the second scene, the spirited eulogy on Drake ... and the fine lines descriptive of the Armada are just such as we might expect from the author of the closing scenes of the second part of *If you know not me, you know nobody*. Heywood was fond of stirring adventures: he is quite at home on the sea.[1]

Based on his own analysis of Heywood's style, and use of couplets, A. M. Clark later agreed with Bullen, noting that 'there seems not to be the slightest doubt that Heywood was the author', and when F. S. Boas stated, in 1950, that 'Bullen's tentative ascription to Heywood has found general acceptance', it seems a new orthodoxy had been established.[2] In 2007 Ronald Bedford et al. noted that the play was 'almost certainly written by Thomas Heywood' and, most recently, William Long accepts Heywood's authorship without question, referring to the play as 'Thomas Heywood's *Dick of Devonshire* (1626?) written by an unknown copier (possibly the playhouse book-keeper) for unknown eyes'.[3] However, despite these confident claims for Heywood, until now no scholarship has yet identified his hand in the play definitively, and attribution has remained speculative, with Robert Davenport, James Shirley, and John Ford all being offered as potential alternatives.[4]

Propitiously, developments in attribution scholarship over the past fifteen years allow the modern researcher to move beyond conjecture. Applying to the play-text the model of computational stylistics championed by Hugh Craig, we are able, for the first time, to demonstrate that Thomas Heywood is, indeed, the likely author of both the main plot and subplot of *Dick of Devonshire*.[5]

Factor analysis of Dick of Devonshire *and Thomas Heywood*
Forty marker words identified by Craig were entered into an index system against each of the characters in *Dick of Devonshire*, and against characters in the available canon of each one of the play-wrights in the authorial frame.[6] The forty marker words were entered into a principal component analysis (PCA), using an 'unrelated' rotation and, following the work of Craig, these were extracted into two principal factors or components. As explained by Craig, with reference to his own data-modelling, but also applicable here,

> Each character in the set is given two scores, one for the first principal component, and one for the second principal component, Each score derives from the character's count on the first words – how many instances of *the*, of *my*, of *would*, etc. – with the counts weighed in one way for the first principal component and another way for the second principal component. What we are looking at in the graph is a form of 'data reduction'. A distillation of all the patterns of fluctuation in the various counts. We start with forty dimensions, one for each of the word-variables, and PCA allows us to project these forty dimensions onto two, and it is this projection that appears in the graph.[7]

The results of the PCA were plotted on to a scattergraph (Figure 1). Characters from *Dick of Devonshire* (n = 28) are displayed as stars and characters from plays with Heywood as sole author (n = 92) are shown as circles.

With the exception of one outlying character from *Dick of Devonshire* (in the top right of the graph), namely Jewell, both the *Dick of Devonshire* and the Heywood set occupy the same area of the scattergraph, suggesting that they originate from the same authorial cluster as each other. In Craig's graph, which plots characters from the Fletcher canon against characters from the Shakespeare canon, Craig was able to draw a dividing line between 'Fletcher' and 'Shakespeare' areas, demonstrating two clear authorial clusters. It is not possible, in the graph plotting *Dick of Devonshire* characters against characters in the Heywood canon, to make any such division. In other words, the characters in the *Dick of Devonshire* set (including characters from both the main and the subplot) were written by

INTRODUCTION

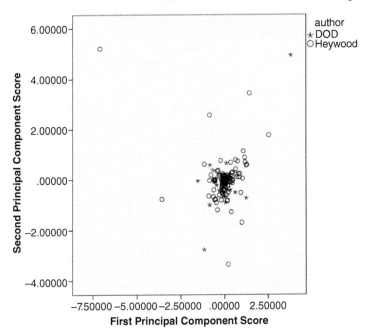

Figure 1 Factor analysis of *Dick of Devonshire* and plays written solely by Thomas Heywood

the same person as the characters in the Heywood set, that person being Thomas Heywood.

DATE AND SOURCES

The only existing textual witness of *Dick of Devonshire*, in MS Egerton 1994, is undated and there is no corresponding entry in the records of the Office of the Revels to provide a timeline for the creation of the play. Similarly, the play remained unprinted until the late nineteenth century, so there is no contemporary entry in the Stationers' Register by which to date the play. However, the topicality of the play's subject material enables us to draw some general conclusions about when it was written. The Cadiz expedition set sail on 8 October 1625. Richard Peeke tells us himself in his pamphlet *Three to One: Being, an English-Spanish Combat* that following

4   DICK OF DEVONSHIRE

his release from the Spanish prison, he 'landed on the three and twenty day of April, 1626, at Foy in Cornwall' (sig. Ev).[8] He had an audience with the King on 18 May 1626, and his autobiographical pamphlet was entered into the Stationers' Register on 18 July 1626 (although it is possible that the pamphlet was circulating before this time). It is likely that Heywood began work on the play around this time; in any event, the play draws heavily on the content of the pamphlet for its main plot, so the play would not have preceded the pamphlet. As the Malone edition observes, 'it might be expected that a play celebrating Peeke's adventures would be written before the end of 1626 and performed before the hero should be forgotten'.[9] Assuming that this is correct (and there is no evidence to make us doubt that it is), *Dick of Devonshire* must have been written in the second half of 1626. If the play was intended for production in an indoor playhouse, as the inclusion of a stage direction calling for cornets to open Act 2 would seem to indicate (see 'Theatrical History', below), a winter performance seems timely, suggesting a performance in late 1626 or early 1627 at the earliest. In the event, it seems that the performance did not take place, but the potential for this is nevertheless useful in identifying the likely chronology of the play's production.

As noted, the play dramatises the ill-fated Cadiz expedition of 1625. The expedition itself is recorded in a number of different sources, from official records to ballads, many of which are captured in the Calendars of State Papers, both Domestic and Venetian.[10] In addition, three first-person accounts offer three discrete perspectives on the expedition: first, the Lord Admiral of the Fleet, Edward Cecil, offered a retrospective justification of the many shortcomings of the trip, placing the blame on everyone except himself; second, the Secretary to the Council of War, Sir John Glanville, recorded each day's events meticulously in his official diary, offering a factual account of every stage of the operation; third, as we have seen, a soldier from the fleet, Richard Peeke, penned *Three to One: Being, an English-Spanish Combat*, relating an entertaining account of the voyage as he experienced it.[11] His is a heroic tale of swashbuckling bravery, far removed from the cold, factual tones of Glanville's diary or the wheedling evasiveness employed by Cecil. Little wonder, then, that Peeke's colourful account should form the primary source material of *Dick of Devonshire*.

Dick of Devonshire follows Peeke's prose narrative very closely, and the majority of the play's dialogue is almost identical to Peeke's

INTRODUCTION

Figure 2 Title page woodcut of Richard Peeke's *Three to One* © Huntington Library, San Marino, California

DICK OF DEVONSHIRE

original account. In a small but significant departure from the prose account, however, the eponymous hero is named Richard Pike. It might be tempting to dismiss this as a simple spelling variant (though the *Oxford English Dictionary* does not list 'peeke' as a variant spelling of 'pike'). However, by changing the central character's name, the play draws upon the soldier's celebrated quarterstaff victory, which forms the climax of the action, aligning the character overtly with his weapon. This name-change might have been inspired by Peeke's self-effacing declaration in the opening pages of his prose account that 'My Present Being consisteth altogether upon the Soldier, (blunt, plaine, and unpolished); so must my Writings be, proceeding from fingers *fitter for the Pike* then the Pen' (emphasis mine). The correspondence of the soldier and his weapon occurs again later in the pamphlet, when Peeke is passed a make-do quarterstaff which is, in fact, 'the head of a Halbert, which went with a Screw, was taken off, and the Steall delivered to me; the other But-end of the Staffe having a Short Iron Pike in it. This was my armor, and in my place I stood, expecting an Opponent' (sig. D2r).

Peeke's autobiographical narrative was not the only document to tell his story. On 19 May 1626 a London rector, Dr Meddus, wrote in a letter to the Revd Mead that

> yesterday being Holy Thursday, one Pyke, a common soldier, left behind the fleet at Cadiz, delivered a challenge to the Duke of Buckingham from the Marquis of ..., brother-in-law to the Conde d'Olivares, in defence of the honour of his sister.[12]

The letter proceeds to describe how 'this Pyke, a Devonshire man, being presented prisoner to the Duke of Medina' was 'offered with a quarterstaff to fight with three rapier men, all of which he vanquished and disarmed'. Meddus and Mead were in constant contact throughout the 1620s, updating each other on recent events, and the inclusion of Peeke's story in their correspondence suggests that they, at least, considered it newsworthy.

A political pamphlet, *A true relation of a brave English stratagem*, printed by Mercurius Britannicus in May 1626 includes the tale of 'one young Merchant, armed only with his Sword and a Spanish Pike' who 'by three adversaries was boldly and resolutely charged'. The similarity of this account to that of Peeke's own prose account is striking. It describes the episode thus:

> That if it pleased the Governour to give him leave, hee himselfe would undertake, (making choise of his Weapon) to fight singly against three of

INTRODUCTION 7

the proudest Champions they would produce against him; to cut off
Circumstance, the Chalenge was accepted, the Governour prepared the
combatants, with the time and place appointed: a great confluence of
people assembled: where one young Merchant, armed onely with his
Sword and Spanish Pike in the lists appeared, who by the three adversaries
was boldly and resolutely charged: but God and his good Cause defended
him so well, that the Combate continued not long, and having received
from them some few scratches, with the losse of a small quantitie of blood,
but without danger, hee so actively and resolutely behaved himselfe
against the survivors, that they after divers wounds from him received
begin to quaile in their former courage, and fight more faintly and further
off, which the Governour perceiving, commanded the Combat to cease.[13]

The story of one man in combat with three assailants is clearly the
same as those set out in Mead's letter and Peeke's pamphlet, and
dramatised in *Dick of Devonshire*. However, there are also significant
differences between this account and Peeke's own account, apparent anomalies which require further consideration. The tale, for
example, is said to originate 'in *Lisbone* not long since' rather than
in Cadiz, and the hero is said to be 'a young Marchant (who for
divers respects desires to have his name concealed)'. In a letter to
Sir Martin Stuteville of Dalham Hall, Mead notes that the English
fleet 'came down the shore to Lisbon' before it reached Cadiz, so this
location does not fall outside the realms of possibility.[14] Similarly, it
is true that a large proportion of the English flotilla bound for Cadiz
comprised merchant ships. Roger Manning estimates that 'naval
ships totalled only thirteen of the nearly one hundred vessels in the
Cadiz fleet, which consisted mostly of merchantmen and Newcastle
colliers'.[15] However, the Cadiz expedition is not mentioned at all in
A true relation, which one might expect in the wider context of the
pamphlet, given the focus on 'remarkeable accidents betweene the
English and Spaniards' noted in its title. Neither is there any suggestion that the merchant completed his feat of single-handed combat
while a prisoner of war. Furthermore, we know that Richard Peeke
was a soldier rather than a merchant; Peeke introduces himself in
his own pamphlet as a man who knows 'a good Shippe ... and a
poore Cabbin and the language of a Cannon', further adding that
he had 'seene the Beginning and End of *Argeires* Voyage', the 1621
expedition commissioned by James I to destroy the strongholds
of pirates off the North African coast. Nor does it ring true that
the man who, in the same year as the above account, produced a
comprehensive pamphlet in which he styled himself as a war hero

8   DICK OF DEVONSHIRE

would request that his name should be withheld in recounting the story.

A true relation differs significantly from *Dick of Devonshire* and Peeke's pamphlet in the way the tale ends:

> Where calling him up to him conveyed him safe to his house, and after much commendation of his valour, very nobly secured him to his Ship, wishing him for his owne safety to be seene no more ashoare. (sig. B3r)

It is not easy to reconcile this version with Peeke's own tale of a release from prison, an audience with the Spanish king, and gifts of 'a Chayne of Gold, and two Jewells for my Wife, and other pretty Thinges for my Children'. Why should there be so much discrepancy between the two versions of the story? The clue lies at the very end of Peeke's own pamphlet, in which he describes what happened to him once he had left Spain.

> Having thus left *Spaine*, I took my way through some part of *France*; Where, by occasion, happening into Company of seven *Spaniards*, their tongues were too lavish in Speeches against our Nation; Upon which some high words flying up and downe the Roome, I leaped from the Table and drew. One of the *Spaniards* did the like (none of the rest being Weaponed, which was more than I knew.) Upon the noise of this Bustling, two *English* Men more came in, Who understanding the Abuses offered to our Countrey. The *Spaniards* in a short time, Recanted on the Knees their Rashnesse. (sigs. D4v–E1r)

One of the Englishmen who enter this scene would appear to be the source of the report set out in the Mercurius account, even if he is not necessarily its author. While the venue is wrong, the location being France instead of Lisbon, the account in *A true relation* resembles Peeke's own postscript closely enough to suggest that both accounts report on the same encounter. If Peeke had enough time to travel from Spain to France, then so had the news of his single-handed defeat of three Spanish soldiers. Peeke's reluctance to reveal his true identity is more readily understandable, then, if he feared the Spaniards' possible reaction to his recent exploits. Indeed, as Glanville observed in a journal entry on 22 October 1625, 'nothing of importance is publiquely done but the Spaniard hath intelligence of it with all speede possible'.[16]

It is important to recognise that, although both accounts appeared in print in the same year, logistics suggest that they were, in all likelihood, written independently of one another. Both accounts were written and printed at approximately the same time, May or June

INTRODUCTION 9

1626. For either to have inspired the other, the respective authors would have needed access to the other's manuscript copy, a possibility that remains unsupported by any extant evidence. Neither are there any verbal parallels between the two documents. Instead, it would appear that the two accounts are an illuminating illustration of the way in which news spread by word of mouth from different sources.

THE PLAY

The main plot of *Dick of Devonshire* tells the story of a Tavistock soldier, Richard Pike, a foot-soldier in the Cadiz expedition of 1625. Pike arrives in Cadiz with the rest of the fleet, and they besiege the fort. While out walking, Pike meets two fellow English soldiers who direct him to a lemon grove that he believes, wrongly, to be in English hands. When Pike reaches the grove, he discovers his countrymen wounded and dying. He stops to help them, but is himself ambushed by Don John, a Spanish lord, and his soldiers. They fight, and Pike has the upper hand. He spares Don John's life, but is rewarded only by being attacked once more by Don John and taken prisoner. Don John's wife, Catelina, brings Pike clothing and food in prison, much to Don John's displeasure; Don John views Catelina's hospitality as a betrayal of both her country and her marital bed. At his trial, Pike is invited to show his martial prowess against three Spanish soldiers. He accepts the invitation, on the condition that he can fight with a weapon of his choosing. Opting for the humble quarterstaff, Pike proceeds to fight off, and defeat, the three soldiers single-handedly, and is celebrated by the Spanish court for his valour. He receives a royal pardon and is offered Spanish citizenship, but declines, declaring his allegiance instead to Charles I and England. He is freed to return home, bestowed with gold and silk by the Spanish court.

The main plot of the play is largely faithful to the source pamphlet's version of events and the majority of the play's dialogue is almost identical to Peeke's original account. However, the play is not consistent in its balance between textual fidelity and dramatic effect. There are some occasions in the play in which Heywood appears to exercise a degree of artistic licence in the staged portrayal of the events set out in the pamphlet to increase their dramatic impact. When Peeke first goes ashore, for example, in the pamphlet version of events, he discovers the bodies of three fellow soldiers, 'starke dead, being slayne, lying in the way' (sig. B4r). A fourth soldier lies wounded, with injuries so severe that Peeke shoots him to end his suffering. In the play, Pike too comes across these bodies, but the shooting is enacted on the stage before Pike's entrance, to provide spectacle for the audience. The stage direction reads, 'Three or four shots discharged. Two soldiers slain, the other falls on his belly' (2.4). The prose account does not specify how the soldiers were killed, and there is nothing to suggest that the killing happened immediately before Peeke came across the bodies. On the stage, however, a whole vignette has been created for dramatic effect. The fact that the shots ring out shortly before Pike's entrance heightens the danger that Pike himself is in, by emphasising the close and deadly proximity of the enemy.

Pike's incarceration as a prisoner of war is also given a great deal more attention in the play than in the prose account. In the pamphlet, Peeke dedicates only five lines to the eighteen days he spends in the Spanish prison. In the play, an entire scene is dedicated to the episode. Pike is visited by Catelina, the wife of Don John. Catelina thanks Pike for sparing her husband's life during their earlier fight, and brings him clothes, food, and money, imploring the jailer to ensure that Pike is treated well. Heywood uses hospitality throughout his work to consider structures of authority and control. In *A Woman Killed with Kindness*, for example, Anne Frankford's decision to fast, therefore refusing the expected provision of food, undermines the patriarchal systems of control her husband uses to normalise relational power structures within the household.[17] Later, in *The Late Lancashire Witches*, written with Richard Brome in 1634, Heywood affirms these relational power structures through a series of invitations to dine, and reputations in the play are made or broken based on the success or otherwise of the subsequent feasts. It is no accident that the eponymous witches choose a wedding feast as the site of their bewitchment, disrupting not only the patriarchal structures of the marriage ritual, but also the hospitality of the extravagant wedding breakfast. Catelina's offer of food and clothing in *Dick of Devonshire*, therefore, normalises the power dynamics of the captor–prisoner relationship, but relieves them of the aggression we might expect in the context of military imprisonment.

The character of Catelina does not appear in the prose account: she acts as a dramatic device whose display of hospitality leads the audience to question their preconceptions about the Spanish. When faced with Pike's initial apprehension, she says,

INTRODUCTION 11

Good sir, let no mistrust of my just purpose
Cross your affection; did you know my love
To honour and to honest actions, you
Would not then reject my gratulations. (3.2.68–71)

The play is ambivalent in its approach to Anglo-Spanish relations, and the introduction of Catelina in this fictitious, or at least speculative, scene is one of the channels through which the relationship between the two countries can be explored. Pike's acceptance of Catelina's hospitality is just one example of the complex way in which the English and the Spanish are represented.

Hence, incidents that are conflated in the prose account appear to be given far more weight in the play. Some of those events that are understated in Peeke's original report are purposefully expanded and explored in more detail on the stage, either with a view to dramatic spectacle or to explore some of the more complex themes of the play. Conversely, there are events in the pamphlet that would provide opportunities for dramatic effect onstage, but which in the play are reported by the character of Pike rather than acted out physically. When relating how he was led to prison, for example, Peeke describes a scene of jeering crowds:

> In my being ledde thus along the Streets, A *Flemming* spying me, cryde out alowde; Whither doe you leade this English *Dogge*. Kill him, kill him, hee's no Christian. And with that, breaking through the Croude, in upon those who held mee, ranne me into the Body with a Halbert, at the Reynes of my Backe, at the least four inches. (sig. C1v)

Considering the extent to which speech and action described in other sections of the pamphlet have been transferred into the dramatic text, particularly relating to Peeke's imprisonment and capture, this episode would seem to be one that would work well on the stage, containing spectacle and heightened emotion in the jeering crowds, and theatrical tension in the halberd attack. Instead, however, Pike simply reports the incident to the Governor as an explanation of the hardships he has suffered in Spain since being attacked by Don John. Like other episodes considered above, the account Pike gives Fernando is taken verbatim from Peeke's report in the pamphlet, but Fernando's dismissive response, 'Poor man, I pity thee, but to the prison with him' (2.5.102), is similarly reflective of a strange reluctance to engage with the episode. While there might have been pragmatic reasons that materially limited the staging of this scene, such as the playhouse's capacity to accommodate the number of players to constitute a crowd, this might be another example of a wider reluctance in the play to portray Spanish characters, however minor, in a wholly negative light.

Confirmation that we can now attribute the play with confidence to the pen of Heywood problematises the playwright's rationale for reproducing, so faithfully, the content of Peeke's pamphlet in the text of *Dick of Devonshire*. Barring the few examples listed above, this near-verbatim approach would have limited Heywood significantly in terms of his own theatrical practice, a practice which, as Rowland has noted, 'rarely observed prescriptive controls'.[18] Unless we dismiss *Dick of Devonshire* as a lazy attempt by Heywood to produce a quick commercial 'win', a dismissal for which there is no evidence, this textual fidelity makes more sense, in a playwright of Heywood's experience, if we consider the main plot to be a straightforward populist adaptation that frees Heywood to experiment, in the subplot, with the innovation of form that he would return to with vigour in writing *The English Traveller* the following year.[19]

Dick of Devonshire's subplot, at first glance, has no connection with the main plot, other than that its antagonist is taken to the same trial as Pike at the play's denouement. The main action of the subplot takes place in the Gusman household. Don Pedro Gusman, his eldest son Manuell, and Don Fernando are departing Cadiz for France, leaving Don Fernando's daughter, Eleonore, in the protection of her fiancé, Gusman's youngest son Henrico, and Henrico's manservant, Buzzano, in the Gusman property. When Henrico tries to convince Eleonore to have sexual intercourse with him, she refuses. Henrico's attempts to persuade her that her honour will not be compromised, because they are already betrothed to one another, fail and Henrico rapes Eleonore. Buzzano overhears the rape, and guesses what has happened when he sees Eleonore, 'loose haired and weeping', but Henrico compels his silence. Eleonore writes to her future father-in-law, Don Pedro, to tell him what has happened. Don Pedro is distraught, but Manuell is less believing of the allegations against his brother, and returns to Cadiz to investigate further. On his return, he discovers that Henrico has, indeed, raped Eleonore. However, Henrico launches a counterattack by accusing Manuell of murdering their father. Both brothers are taken to trial (at the same sessions as Pike in the main plot), and both plead their innocence. Unbeknown to the brothers, Don Pedro has returned for the trial, and disguises himself as a friar, revealing his true identity only after hearing Henrico's attempt to falsely condemn Manuell.

INTRODUCTION 13

Manuell is acquitted, and both the father and Eleonore (albeit after some coercion by the Lords) forgive Henrico for the rape, and order is restored once more.

Jeremy Lopez considers the order in which the two plots may have been written:

> 'It is a curious and characteristic thing,' says J. Brooking Rowe, editor of the play's most recent modern-spelling edition, that the playwright 'brings in the adventures of Peeke to give title and English interest to a romantic drama with which they have scarcely the remotest connection' (ix). This seems to imagine the impetus for composition exactly backward: surely the Peeke material was what cried out for dramatization, and onto this the author grafted a romantic plot that he had already in progress or that he concocted for the purpose.[20]

Neither of the above imaginings of impetus is quite sufficient. As is the case with most of the sparse existing critical response to *Dick of Devonshire*, both negate the relevance of the subplot, dismissing it either as something that needs to have English interest brought to it, or something that was 'grafted' on to the main plot. However, the subplot was more than a random time-filler. When the play is considered within the context and chronology of Heywood's body of work, the subplot of *Dick of Devonshire* can be seen as the playground in which Heywood experimented with ideas of form that, when developed more fully the following year, would mark out its successor, *The English Traveller*, as what Rowland has called 'a play concerned with the instability of generic conventions, and yet [...] also one which confidently insists on its capacity to amuse and disturb in the same breath'.[21]

THE TEXT

The one remaining textual witness of *Dick of Devonshire*, and the copy-text for the present edition, is the second of a number of plays bound up in MS Egerton 1994.[22] A series of pinholes on the left hand side of the page indicates that it once stood alone as a document in its own right, with a stitched binding. While scholars agree that the script was prepared by a scribe, there has been some debate among the few who have explored the manuscript in any detail as to the manuscript's purpose. W. W. Greg concluded that the text was prepared for private use, particularly because of the Latin motto on its title page. This argument was echoed by G. E. Bentley

14 DICK OF DEVONSHIRE

and appeared to have been strengthened when the same scribal hand was detected in a manuscript verse miscellany in the 1630s.[23] However, it seems unlikely that the manuscript was intended for a private readership, particularly in light of the lack of evidence to suggest performance. It would have been very unusual for somebody to commission a private dramatic transcript for a play that had not previously been a success in the playhouse. Indeed, as Samuel Chappuzeau noted in 1674,

> A play, however excellent, if it has not been performed, cannot find a Bookseller to undertake its printing; and the least thing scrawled on paper, if it pleased in the Theatre, will immediately find a merchant.[24]

There is far more evidence to suggest that the extant *Dick of Devonshire* witness was intended for use in the playhouse, even if this intention was not fulfilled. The manuscript is a folio, which suggests it was prepared as a working document rather than a private transcript, which we would expect to be a quarto, like the Malone manuscript of *A Game at Chess*.[25] Moreover, as the Malone Society edition of *Dick of Devonshire* notes, evidence suggests that the scribe behind the folio was probably a playhouse scribe.[26] His hand has been detected in insertions to the transcript of Middleton's 1602 play *Blurt Master Constable*, and closer investigation shows that the text the scribe amended in *Blurt* was not simply copied out of the version in the printed quarto, implying that he must have had access to a theatrical manuscript. In both *Dick of Devonshire* and *Blurt Master Constable*, speech prefixes are surrounded by ruled lines when they occur in the centre of the page; stage directions are centred and again boxed in with ruled lines to distinguish them from the dialogue. The same scribal hand also produced two leaves, the title page, and the first sixty lines of Chapman's 1611 play *May Day*. Therefore, it appears that by 1626, the probable date of the transcription of the *Dick of Devonshire* manuscript, he was adept at working with play-texts.

The materiality of the manuscript itself and its provenance also suggest a theatrical rather than a literary origin. James McManaway observes that, while invisible to the naked eye, photostats of the script show that the leaves of the folio have been folded in the way common to manuscripts intended for playhouse use.[27] In addition, the stitched binding was a familiar method employed in prompt books and playhouse manuscripts. Finally, the fact that the manuscript of *Dick of Devonshire* was at one time owned by the player

INTRODUCTION 15

and theatre manager William Cartwright the Younger adds weight to the probability of a theatrical provenance. Cartwright had been involved with Christopher Beeston's Queen Henrietta Maria's Men, and Beeston is known to have been a long-time friend and colleague of Heywood's, which might provide a channel of mutual acquaintance through which Cartwright acquired the manuscript of *Dick of Devonshire*. Although Cartwright was a bookseller in later life, his bequest to Dulwich College, which included the manuscript of *Dick of Devonshire* together with the other papers bound in MS Egerton 1994, probably related to the many manuscripts he had accumulated during an active life in the theatre, as the bequest was not classified as surplus stock but rather comprised items from his own personal collection. Indeed, the inventory of bequeathed books lists 'stitched and covered books' alongside other 'Bookes Richly bound of great value'. As Eleanore Boswell notes, 'stitched and covered books' was an accurate description of manuscript prompt books, though Boswell prefers instead to think the description referred to 'a printed book stitched into a paper cover but unbound'.[28] Given that scholarship has demonstrated only a limited market for commercial transcripts, together with the fact that the manuscript of *Dick of Devonshire* clearly displays needle holes along the spine, indicating stitching, it seems likely that the transcript was, in fact, prepared for theatrical use.

Scholarship on the various documents that would have been produced for use in the Jacobean and Caroline playhouse, together with detailed textual analyses of early modern plays with a greater number of extant witnesses, has made it possible to speculate where on a stemma the extant *Dick of Devonshire* manuscript would sit.[29] Speculation about the early stages of the 'writing' process, of which we have no documentary evidence, provides an unstable base from which to further the discussion. Nevertheless, it is possible to draw some conclusions about lost manuscripts that must have existed in order for these extant transcripts to have been produced. Any clues that enable us to trace back from the extant manuscripts to possible sources or earlier copies are of fundamental importance in considering how manuscript play-texts might have been used in the playhouse in the time leading up to and during the play's intended period of performance. Therefore, the concrete information that exists must be supplemented by some level of informed conjecture.

The limited commercial market for plays in manuscript and the likely minimal demand for the text of an unperformed play means

16 DICK OF DEVONSHIRE

that the play does not fit comfortably alongside the manuscripts intended for private or commercial use outside the playhouse. Instead, it fits within the group of documents prepared for use in the playhouse. This group would comprise, at a minimum, the original authorial copy, which Gary Taylor refers to as the pre-script (literally the manuscript which precedes the script used at the time of the performance), and the prompt book, which would normally be the version of the play forwarded to the Office of the Revels for licensing.[30] If a separate document were submitted to the Office of the Revels, this would also have to be accounted for in the stemma. In addition to the pre-script and the prompt book, the third and final set of play manuscripts that would have been required in the playhouse, if the play were to be performed, relates to the pieces of text that the actors themselves would have engaged with directly. Once the play had been licensed, a number of smaller manuscripts would have been created to provide an overall plot for the play and the separate cues and parts for the players.

William Long suggests that the extant manuscript of *Dick of Devonshire* was copied from 'the playhouse copy as prepared for production by the company bookkeeper', in other words, the prompt book.[31] Having conducted a comprehensive comparison with the eighteen remaining extant examples of manuscript playbooks, Long concludes that MS Egerton 1994 follows some of the conventions detectable in extant playbooks, namely the centring of the dialogue and the placement of stage directions and speech prefixes. However, Long also identifies that MS Egerton 1994 differs from the extant playbooks in two significant ways: first, there is an absence of white space around the text (and subsequent boxing of stage directions) which would be expected in a playbook to enable the copying out of parts; and second, changes of speaker are not indicated by a new line, as would be expected, but are rather run together, again to save space.[32] As there is no apparent reason why the playbook of *Dick of Devonshire* should break the convention of other early modern playbooks, at least as detectable in the small number of extant examples, Long's proposal that MS Egerton 1994 was copied from the prompt book is convincing.

If the copy-text for the extant MS Egerton 1994 is not the theatre playbook itself, this, in turn, raises a number of questions that we may never be able to answer beyond conjecture. As noted above, the play is not listed in the extant fragments of the licence records of the then Master of the Revels, Henry Herbert, and does not seem

INTRODUCTION 17

to have been performed contemporarily. Therefore the prompt book that we would expect to be submitted for licensing was possibly incomplete and either lost or, indeed, not produced at all, which would negate it as a candidate for the copy-text of MS Egerton 1994. Were evidence of a prompt book to be found, the fact that there is no record of the play's performance leaves the playhouse scribe's motive for making a further copy of the obsolete prompt book unclear. Perhaps we should not rule out the possibility that, instead, the extant manuscript was derived closely from the pre-script, perhaps as closely as a direct copy. While the predominance of the scribal hand and the clean nature of the copy indicate that it was not the pre-script itself, logic rules that this pre-script must have been the common ancestor of any later manuscripts.

THEATRICAL HISTORY

There is no evidence to support a performance of *Dick of Devonshire*, either at the time it was written or, indeed, at any time since. While Bedford et al. state that '[Richard] Pike's adventures quickly made it to the popular stage', setting out the play's appeal 'to playgoers', the existence of the dramatic manuscript appears to have been misinterpreted as evidence of its staging, because, in fact, no textual trace of a performance has yet been found.[33] While Richard Peeke's own exploits are cited by contemporary men of letters, poets, and pamphleteers, there are no similar references to the play bearing his name.[34] The Malone edition argues that 'if [*Dick of Devonshire*] never reached the stage, this may have been due to the favourable portrayal of Spanish chivalry at a time when England was being prepared for war with Spain', while A. J. Hoenselaars adds that 'the play is not sufficiently pro-English'.[35] However, the argument that the play was somehow unpatriotic in shining a light on the unmitigated disaster of the Cadiz expedition becomes problematic when considering that both Peeke and Cecil contemporaneously published their own accounts of the same expedition without detriment.

While no record of a performance has been found, there is little doubt, as set out above, that the manuscript was prepared for the purposes of performance. As such, it provides tantalising fragments of evidence about the potential players' company intended to stage *Dick of Devonshire*. As noted above, we know that the manuscript was owned at one time by William Cartwright the Younger. Cartwright had associations with a number of playing companies. He

18   DICK OF DEVONSHIRE

acted with both the King and Queen of Bohemia's Men at Salisbury Court from 1629, and, later, Queen Henrietta Maria's Men. During the Restoration period he became a shareholder in the King's Company.[36] Therefore, the *Dick of Devonshire* manuscript bequeathed to Dulwich College could reasonably have resided with any one of these companies originally. Additionally, as the Malone edition observes, 'MS Egerton 1994 does not … represent part of the library of a particular company but is a collection of plays brought together from sources and for purposes unknown'.[37] Indeed, the collection includes plays that were performed variously by Lady Elizabeth's players, Prince Charles's players, and the Queen Anne's Players of the Revels, all of which must also enter the frame if we are to use Cartwright's own affiliation as the single determinant. However, two further details point to a possible resolution: the identification of the author, Heywood, and the playhouse for which he wrote.

The manuscript contains indicators that the play was intended for performance in an indoor playhouse. The play requires no large crowd scenes, no cannons, nor hell mouth. While battle scenes are implied, the audience sees no fighting of the scale that would necessitate the larger stage of the amphitheatre. The stage direction opening Act 2, for example, calls for '*Alarum; as the soft music begins, a peal of ordnance goes off; then cornets sound a battle*' (2.1). By 1626–27 cornets, which had originally characterised productions by children's companies, had been brought into the indoor playhouses to signify military action in a smaller arena.[38] There is no evidence that cornets were used in military contexts in amphitheatres. The only two other plays known to include stage directions requiring cornets to sound a battle, *Antonio and Mellida* and *The Dumb Knight*, were written for indoor playhouses, namely Paul's and Whitefriars, respectively.[39] In late 1626–27, the likely intended timeframe for performance, there were only two indoor playhouses: the second Blackfriars and the Cockpit (also known as the Phoenix). Salisbury Court would not open for another three years. There is no evidence that a Heywood play had ever been produced in the Blackfriars before 1626, nor had he written for its resident company, the Kings Men, before.[40] Therefore, it seems unlikely that *Dick of Devonshire* would have been intended to play there. In contrast, Heywood wrote *The Captives* for Queen Elizabeth's Men in 1624 (the company that would form the basis of Queen Henrietta Maria's Men the following year) and Queen Henrietta Maria's Men staged at least three of Heywood's plays between 1625 and 1630.[41] We know that

INTRODUCTION 19

William Cartwright also acted with Queen Henrietta Maria's Men, albeit later than Heywood's association with the company, providing a possible explanation as to how *Dick of Devonshire* assumed its place in MS Egerton 1994. From a consideration of the available evidence, therefore, it appears most likely that Heywood wrote *Dick of Devonshire* for Queen Henrietta Maria's Men, intending the play to be performed in the company's resident playhouse, the Cockpit, owned and managed by Heywood's long-time colleague, Christopher Beeston.

STAGECRAFT

In February 1602/3 Philip Henslowe recorded in his diary that he paid a tailor 22 shillings 'for velluet & satten for the womon gowne of black veluett with the other lyneges belonginge to it' and the next day reimbursed Heywood £6 and 13 shillings 'for A womones gowne of black veluett for the playe of A womon kylled with kyndness'.[42] Heywood had bought the costume for the main character of his play a month before the play was finished, demonstrating, as Grace Ioppolo notes, that from relatively early in his career he was closely involved in the detail of the practical production of his work.[43] Similarly, Richard Rowland posits that

> For anyone interested in discovering, or recapturing, the essence of Heywood's theatre, the 'book of the play' [...] cannot alone provide a reliable guide. This is of course the case with all drama of the past, but I would suggest that the difficulty of establishing the relationship between text and performance is perhaps more acute with Heywood than it is with any of his contemporaries.[44]

Therefore, while evidence of a contemporary performance of *Dick of Devonshire* eludes us, nevertheless, given that we do have evidence of the attention Heywood usually paid to the pragmatics of the theatrical production of his work, it would be remiss to ignore the traces of stagecraft detectable within the extant manuscript.

As the early modern period progressed, the cultural significance attached to clothing offstage began to move in two opposing directions, one in which each item of clothing upheld a set of deep-rooted, traditional values and related connotations, the very essence of the person wearing it; and one in which clothing obtained a transient quality, evolving with changing fashions, and therefore without the traditional implications of the former. Onstage, this opposition was brought together by the players and the audience. On the one hand, plays reflected the idea of an identity created by costume, an identity extending beyond the garment itself to a set of associated qualities and implications for social status. When Catelina offers Don John's clothes to the imprisoned Richard Pike in *Dick of Devonshire*, Don John's condemnation of the gesture as 'treason to my bed' not only refers to his wife's betrayal of him personally as she offers support to the enemy, but also links to the belief that by wearing Don John's clothes, Pike would in some way assume the authority invested in them; therefore, Catelina is instigating a treacherous act, undermining the rule of the Spanish colonel and assisting the triumph of the English soldier.

On the other hand, the emerging transience of clothing as a fashion item could be detected within a contingent of the playhouse audience, as certain individuals attended the theatre so as to be seen in their attire. Dekker encouraged dandy playgoers to be seated on the stage, advising that 'It is fit that hée, whom the most tailors bils do make roome for, when he comes should not be basely (like a vyoll) casd up in a corner'.[45] As garments assumed increasing transience with changing fashion, so the figure of the tailor, the creator of such garments, was portrayed as morally suspect, with greater concern for making money than for the practicality of the clothing. *Dick of Devonshire*'s Buzzano declares that 'tailors are the wittiest knaves that live by bread' because 'for every body now looks so narrowly to tailor's bills ... that the needle lance knights in revenge of those prying eyes, put so many hooks and eyes to every hose and doublet.' (4.1.110–13). The tailors, the 'needle lance knights', are adding superfluous fastenings to increase their bill.

Heywood uses costume to play with the customary tradition of the stock character, undermining the expectations of both the characters in the play and the audience. Adopting a costume at odds with a character's perceived or expected personality or status was a popular device in early modern drama. In Dekker's *Match Me in London*, for instance, performed in 1611 and relicensed by Herbert in 1623, Malevento states of Cordolente: 'Too well thou hast undone me, / Thou art a Civill Theefe with lookes demure / As is thy habit, but a Villaine's heart'. Similarly, in *A Game at Chess*, the White King's Pawn proclaims, 'You see my outside, but you know my heart, Knight / Great difference in the colour' (1.1.313–14). Instances in which the person and the apparel are at odds are most powerful when the character involved is dressed in religious attire,

INTRODUCTION 21

most commonly a habit. When the character is discovered subsequently to display any behaviour other than the reverend nature inherent in their costume, the betrayal reaches beyond the characters of the play, and beyond the audience, as an attempt to deceive both the Church and God. In *Dick of Devonshire*, upon discovering that the report of his father's death was a lie, Manuell cries 'Such a reverend habit / Should not give harbour to so black a falsehood' (5.1.341–2). The phrase 'reverend habit' was used in several plays of the period. Sometimes, the habit did reflect the perceived virtue of the character: in James Shirley's *The Grateful Servant*, for example, Fox acknowledges that Valentio's 'charity / Make you still worthy of that reverend habit'.[46] More usually, however, and as employed by Heywood, the habit was used in dramatic productions to engage with the concept of evil concealed beneath the sanctity of monastic robes.

Heywood also uses jewellery as a motif throughout *Dick of Devonshire*. In Act 1, scene 2, recalling days of Anglo-Spanish peace, Soldier 1 compares the stability to 'chains of pearl / about the necks of either' (1.2.45–6). However, in later scenes, when Pike has been captured by the Spanish, this image is replaced by an iron shackle around his neck, which the Jailer refers to as 'a new clean ruff band about your necke, of old rusty iron' (4.2.25–6). The transformation of the necklace from pearl into rusty iron metaphorises relations between England and Spain, which have turned from peace to hostility both within the action of the play and the political climate of the period. However, at the end of the play, when the Spanish declare Pike a hero for defeating three men with only a quarterstaff, the original image of the necklace is restored, though 'chains of pearl' are now 'a gold chain' (5.1.311), in the gift that Pike sends home to his wife on his release. The gold of the chain reflects Pike's new elevated status in Spain, invoking perhaps the image of mayoral chains of office, but also materialising the memory of peaceful political relations between the two countries of the first scene.

As the use of staged costume invested a garment with social and moral attributes, so stage properties did the same for material objects. Act 3, scene 3 of *Dick of Devonshire* opens with a stage direction: '*Ent.* DON PEDRO *reading a letter, and* MANUELL'. As the scene progresses, the audience learns that Eleonora has written to Don Pedro to tell him that she has been raped by his son, Henrico. To Don Pedro, the letter takes on monstrous qualities, reflecting the hideousness of its content. He cries, 'this murdering spectacle, this

22   DICK OF DEVONSHIRE

field of paper / stuck all with Basilisks' eyes' (3.3.12–13). The materiality of the letter here is inextricably linked to the content. Further violent imagery follows, as Don Pedro asks, 'does't not seem / like a full cloud of blood ready to burst / and fall upon our heads?' (3.3.14–16), as if the very paper on which the letter is written poses a physical threat to its recipients. Similar words can be found in *The Merchant of Venice*, when Antonio describes a letter he has written: 'The paper as the body of my friend, / And every word in it a gaping wound / Issuing life blood' (3.2.263–5).

The letter here acts as a metaphor for violence and aggression inflicted on the body. The damage inflicted on the body and reflected in writing is a result of the sexual violence of the rape, displaced from Eleonora, the letter-writer, to the letter's recipient. As Howard Marchitello has noted, when corporeal language of this kind is employed, writing becomes 'an act of construction and of destruction, as a hopeful act of preservation and at the same time as an act of absolute violence'.[47] Certainly, despite the fact that the audience does not hear the actual content of Eleonora's letter, paraphrased through Don Pedro as a third party instead, the duality identified by Marchitello can be detected in the letter. Eleonora's cry for help is also a cry for the preservation of her virtue, yet at the same time the person to whom she makes this disclosure is the father of the man she accuses of her rape. Distressed by the ordeal that Eleonora has experienced, but also by the fact that it has been perpetrated by his own son, Don Pedro is doubly affected by the letter. Immediately after reading it, he declares,

> But in this lewd exploit I lose a son
> And thou a brother, my Emanuell,
> And our whole house the glory of her name.
> Her beauteous name, that never was disdained,
> Is, by this beastly fact, made odious. (3.3.26–30)

It is significant that at this time Don Pedro visualises his accused son 'Clad all in flames, with an inscription / Blazing on's head: Henrico the Ravisher?' (3.3.20–1); the writing in flames partially repurifies Eleonora's name while simultaneously damning Henrico's. Thus the letter as performed is a violent force that threatens life, liberty, and reputation.

The person who brought the letter to Don Pedro is not present on the stage; the letter has already been delivered before the scene begins. Because the letter has been delivered 'by the common post'

INTRODUCTION 23

(3.3.34), Manuell refuses to believe its contents, choosing instead to regard the letter as part of conspiracy to split up the family. Manuell reasons that his father, Don Pedro, receives letters every week from 'noble friends', delivered through a private arrangement, none of which relate news of the sort disclosed in Eleonora's letter. Manuell knows Eleonora because she is engaged to his brother, yet, because he does not know the letter bearer, he disregards her allegations. Alan Stewart notes that in early modern drama, letters 'are stolen, lost, forged, opened without permission, read by the wrong person … Letters are often used with a sophisticated twist, which usually tends to undermine stability.'[48] Eleonora's letter does not fulfil any of these stock dramatic devices, and yet Manuell suspects it of most of them. He asserts, 'Some villain hath filled up a cup of poison / T''infect the whole house of the Gusman family' (3.3.43–4). In an illustration of theatricality, the expected stock motif of the staged letter as catalyst for the reader's demise is turned back on itself; Manuell expects the letter to be forged and deceiving, yet it is genuine. Ironically, Manuell accuses Don Pedro of reading too much into the letter when that crime is Manuell's himself: 'Indeed, you take too deep a sense of it' (3.3.17).

If costumes and properties contributed to the visual spectacle of performance, so Heywood also used sound effects and music to merge with both the spectacle and the dialogue to create a multi-dimensional theatrical experience that cannot be appreciated fully through a reading of the play-text. *Dick of Devonshire* celebrates a soldier's heroic success in the face of danger at the hands of the Spanish. The focus of the central plot is military, and Heywood uses sound effects throughout to reflect this, as can be seen in the very first stage direction of the play, in which there is an *'Alarum; as the soft music begins, a peal of ordnance goes off; then cornets sound a battle; which ended, enter* CAPTAIN, Master of a Ship [JEWELL], I SOLDIER, DICK PIKE, *with muskets'* (2.1.SD). The incongruity of these sound effects reflects the unrest that prompts Buzzano to observe that 'they spit fore already' in the previous scene. The cornets serve to emphasise the military aspect, as was their function in the early modern indoor playhouse. In Act 4, scene 3, the climax of the action, the Duke of Macada's order that 'Drums beat all the time they fight' is made manifest by the stage direction *'Drums'* twenty lines later. Both the drums and the cornets would have been familiar dramatic motifs to an early modern audience. Compare, for example, Jonson's *Epicoene*, in which Morose declares 'Nay, I would

24 DICK OF DEVONSHIRE

sit out a play, that were nothing but fights at sea, drum, trumpet, and target' (4.2), highlighting once again the link between drums, trumpets (or cornets), and battle on the early modern stage.

THE OCCASION OF THE PLAY

When *Dick of Devonshire* was written in 1626, England's political climate had shifted significantly from the policy of appeasement with Spain followed by James I. In an attempt to retain their dignity following the failed attempt at securing a marriage alliance with the Spanish Infanta in 1623, Prince Charles and the Duke of Buckingham allied themselves with those clamouring for war, a group that Janet Clare refers to as 'the war party', though it was by no means as organised as this terminology suggests.[49] Charles succeeded James in March 1625. Buckingham retained his position of royal favourite and, with James's diplomatic concerns superseded by those of the new monarch, the duke was free to aid Charles in pursuing a more aggressive foreign policy. A 1626 proclamation reflected the altered relationship between England and its continental neighbours, commanding all coastal residents to remain in their homes, and anybody who had moved away from the coast within the previous year to return, so that if the enemy attempted to land, 'it would bee much easier to repell them, then when they shall be landed and intrenched, or put into Array'.[50]

In May 1625 Buckingham instructed a Council of War to send an Anglo-Dutch fleet to Spain on a mission to secure the occupation of a naval base in the bay of Cadiz, with a view to barricading Spanish trading routes and acquiring an ideal spot from which to raid the annual Spanish treasure fleet. This expedition was planned to mirror an earlier English raid, executed in 1596 and spectacularly successful. As Paul Hammer has shown, the leadership of the original expedition was plagued by personal rivalries, and while the fleet triumphed in the raid on Cadiz itself, the Spanish surprised the English with a counterattack only four months later.[51] However, by 1625 the internal wrangling of the commanders had been forgotten as accounts of the Elizabethan expedition obtained currency as propaganda for those advocating war against Spain. The 1596 expedition appeared as a chapter in Samuel Purchas's 1625 work in four volumes celebrating 'a history of the world, in sea voyages & landetravells, by Englishmen & others'.[52] By 1626 printed reminiscences

INTRODUCTION   25

of a golden age of Elizabethan seafaring included an English translation of a French document dedicated to 'the Right worshipfull Sir Francis Drake, Knight' and Philip Nicholls's *Sir Francis Drake revived*, as well as a number of publications evoking memories of the Earl of Essex.[53] Indeed, as Hammer points out, in 1625 'the stories of Cadiz mingled with those about Drake, Hawkins and Grenville to produce that myth of bold Elizabethan "sea dogs" which contrasted so sharply with the eirenic policies of James I'.[54] A Caroline recreation of this great naval success appeared to provide an ideal opportunity for Charles and Buckingham both to satisfy the calls for war with Spain that had been escalating since 1623, and to banish memories of the humiliating failed marriage alliance.

The Cadiz expedition of 1625 was an unmitigated fiasco, however. Poor discipline among troops and captains, coupled with inadequate provisions, sickness, and a Spanish ambush that wiped out two-thirds of the English soldiers, saw the English fleet limp home defeated rather than in the triumphant blaze of glory that had been anticipated. The failed expedition was seized upon by libellers who delighted in the series of disasters that befell the beleaguered convoy. Indeed, when the Admiral of the Fleet, Sir Edward Cecil, was called to appear before the Privy Council on his return, a London rector, Dr Meddus, reported in a letter that Cecil 'fell into a passion, saying that never man was abused as he; that before his going and since his return, there had been made libels and ballads to his disgrace'.[55] One such libel, *Upon the English fleete sett forth. Anno. 1625*, read as a narrative of the expedition, and made clear that the failures of the expedition were inherent even before the fleet set sail, due to inexperienced leadership:

> And ten thousand foote, were added untoo't
> Which were at Plimouth traynd
> By those that knewe little but to eate up your vittaile
> And that was all they gaind.[56]

From this unfavourable beginning, the verse proceeds to highlight the complete lack of impact that the English troops had in Cadiz:

> Wee landed our men, & marcht too & agen
> Three dayes & then came back
> To our shipps againe, having gotten in Spaine,
> Our bellys full of sacke.
> This service thus ended, wee homewards intended.

Indeed, the insobriety of the soldiers mentioned in this libel became a notorious marker of the expedition, and was acknowledged in the extant journals of both Cecil and the secretary to the Council of War, Sir John Glanville: Cecil noted that 'all the Country was full of wine' and 'there was no keeping of the Soldiers from it', while Glanville was more open in his criticism, condemning soldiers for 'the weakness of their late drunkenness'.[57] The libel concludes by apportioning blame for the failure of the expedition to the commander:

> God blesse charles our Kinge, & every thinge
> That hee warlickly takes in hande.
> And in his next choyse hee shall have my voyce
> For a wiser man to commande.

It is not clear whether the libeller intended the 'wiser man to commande' to replace Cecil or Buckingham; Cecil was second-in-command to Buckingham who, while not part of the Cadiz expedition due to commitments in the Dutch Provinces, had nevertheless given the instructions for the Spanish invasion. Given the nature of other libels on the subject, however, it seems likely that the criticism is aimed at Buckingham. A 1626 libel, *Vox Britanniae Ad Hispaniam*, for example, declares that the English should be more fearful of an enemy within than of the Spanish navy.

> Was there ever knowen, so fyne a trycke to stripe us;
> Spayne lett your roodes alone, wee have enoughe to whip us,
> Of our one.[58]

While Buckingham is not named explicitly, he was increasingly unpopular following the Spanish debacle, and impeachment proceedings were launched against him in the same year as a direct result of the disasters in Cadiz. Thus it seems likely that when encountering the libeller's proclamation that 'heer at home do staye, worse enemyes unto us', the libel's audience would recognise allusions to Buckingham, who was Lord Admiral and, since the autumn of 1624, Warden of the Cinque Ports. The overall impression of the expedition depicted in libellous verse is of sheer ineffectiveness. The analogy of 'a Navye went into Spayne' with 'a Munkye clumbe up a tree' which 'when he fell downe then downe fell hee' was as far removed from the triumphant expedition celebrated in 1596 as could be imagined, and such unfavourable comparisons were posted as libels across London and beyond.[59]

INTRODUCTION 27

ANGLO-SPANISH RELATIONS IN THE PLAY

Perhaps unexpectedly, given the political context in which *Dick of Devonshire* was written, the play provides a nuanced portrayal of its characters. In the same way that Heywood refused to take an anti-Spanish stance in *The Captives*, two years previously, in *Dick of Devonshire*, as A. J. Hoenselaars recognises, Heywood's 'portrayal of the Spaniards – with the exception of Don John and his followers – is surprisingly favourable'.[60] Heywood does not caricature the Spanish as a nation of darkness and dishonesty, as Middleton does in *A Game at Chess*, but instead develops individual characters, each with their own flaws and virtues. Because the play follows its primary source material so closely throughout, occasions on which it does deviate from its sources are all the more conspicuous. It is telling, therefore, that the most significant difference between pamphlet and play is that Heywood omits entirely a graphic account of Spanish violence towards the English, as recorded by Peeke. The English troops were marching to a bridge near Puntal,

> In going up to which, some of our Men were unfortunately and unmanly surprised, and before they knew their own danger, had their Throates cutte; Some having their Braines beaten out with the stockes of Muskets; others, their Noses slic'd off; whilst some Heads were spurned up & downe the Streets like Footeballs, and some Eares worn in scorne in *Spanish* Hattes: For when I was in prison in *Cales* (whether some of these *Spanish Picaroes* were brought in, for flying from the Castle,) I was an eye witnesse, of *English* Mens Eares worne in that despightfull manner. (sigs. B3r–v)

This passage is unusual in the context of the rest of the pamphlet for the extreme violence it describes. It would be understandable if the scene were considered too graphic to be staged (although such violence would not be unique in theatre of the period), but it is strange that there is no reference to it at all. Indeed, the episode is considered noteworthy by Glanville, who records finding 'one of our Soldiers dead with his eares and nose cutt off' in his journal.[61] When, in the play, Pike is imprisoned, he specifies the incident described above, in which he was attacked by the Fleming, but at no point does he mention the slaughter of English troops. While it is true that the main plot of *Dick of Devonshire* concerns itself only with the experiences of the eponymous hero, and while, in the pamphlet, Peeke himself has not ventured on to shore at the time the massacre takes place, nevertheless he claims to have witnessed

Figure 3 Drake's Island, Plymouth (formerly St Nicholas's Island, the 'little island before Plymouth', 4.3.112) © Amy Sampson Photography, 2015

Spaniards in the prison wearing the ears of Englishmen in their hats, a sight that is not acknowledged anywhere in the prison scenes in the play.

Hoenselaars sees this omission as symptomatic of the dramatist's unwillingness to provide an indiscriminate representation of the Spanish as arrogant and cruel.[62] It could be argued, alternatively, that Heywood did not include the episode because it revealed weaknesses in the English side, vulnerabilities that would not be welcomed at a time when England was at war with Spain. This is hinted at in another minor discrepancy between the pamphlet and the play in its pivotal scene. During the account of the quarterstaff challenge in the pamphlet, Peeke admits to 'seeing my selfe faint and wearied, I vowed to my Soule, to doe something, ere she departed from me' (sig. D3r.). Pike acknowledges no such fragility in the play, as if an admission to momentary weakness would devalue the hero's hard-fought victory. However, while there is evidence to suggest that English military failure would not constitute good subject matter in the contemporary political context, nevertheless there is more to support Hoenselaars's theory; most of the incidents showing

INTRODUCTION 29

unpleasant Spanish behaviour in the pamphlet are conspicuous in the play only through their absence.

Despite Heywood's apparently sympathetic treatment of Spanish chivalry, the attitude of the play is far from resolutely pro-Spanish and pro-Catholic. Two particular episodes as depicted in the play have far more anti-Spanish implications than their equivalents in the prose account. Indeed, these are the only occasions when events are reordered and words changed. In both the pamphlet and the play, Peeke/Pike is visited by two Friars the night before his trial, to give him an opportunity to confess his sins ahead of a possible death sentence at the following day's trial. In the pamphlet, following the sequence of questioning detailed above, the Duke of Medina informs Peeke, almost as an afterthought, that the two Friars who offered to hear the prisoner's confession the previous night had been to Plymouth recently to gather intelligence for the Spanish court. The Friars' visit to Peeke's town is underplayed and, once Peeke has been informed, the incident is not mentioned again; the trial continues unabated. In the play, however, the Friars' journey is given a sinister twist, as their prior knowledge of Plymouth is revealed through an aside during Pike's confession and is not mentioned at all during the trial. Unlike the pamphlet, where Peeke is informed of the Friars' alternative role by a figure of authority, the aside makes the disclosure look underhanded, invoking the commonly used motif of the period in which dishonesty was concealed beneath holy robes. Think again of Manuell's cries at 5.1.341–2 upon discovering that the report of his father's death was a lie.

If this was the only instance of anti-Catholic feeling in the play, a suggestion of Hispanophobia would be tenuous. However, there is a further significant difference between the pamphlet and the play that would seem to put this beyond doubt. When, in the pamphlet, Peeke accepts the challenge to demonstrate his combat skills, he declares, 'He was unworthy of the Name of an *English* Man, that should refuse to Fight with one Man of any Nation whatsoever.' The equivalent declaration in the play reads,

> May he be never called an Englishman
> That dares not look a devil in the face. (4.3.168–9)

A 'man of any nation' has been made more specific, aligning nation and religion, and as Pike is about to fight the Spanish soldiers, the implication is that the devil and the Spanish are one and the same. As noted, when the prose and dramatic text are so closely aligned,

30   DICK OF DEVONSHIRE

a deviation like this is significant. On this occasion, Heywood gives the words to Pike himself, the hero of the action. There is nothing else in the play to lead the audience to doubt the validity of his opinions, and so it can only be concluded that the anti-Catholic, anti-Spanish feeling inherent in this seemingly unimportant section of dialogue should be accepted by the audience without challenge.

The Spanish king's invitation to Pike to 'Serve him in his Dominions ... upon a golden pension' is rejected outright, providing further direction to the audience as to where their sympathies should lie. Pike declares,

> (The King of England)
> Let me pay that bond I owe my life
> Of my allegiance. And that being paid,
> There is another obligation; (5.1.285–8)

While Heywood's attitude towards Spain in the play is ambiguous, fluctuating between praise of Spain's hospitality and suspicion of its motives, Pike's words here confirm that its overall commitment is, undeniably, to the English Crown.

THIS EDITION

The Revels edition is based on MS Egerton 1994, fols. 30–51, throughout. The procedures of this edition are those of the Revels Plays generally. Spelling has been modernised throughout, unless to do so would compromise the rhythm of the metre. The punctuation of MS Egerton 1994 has been modernised.

The borders between verse and prose passages of MS Egerton 1994 have been retained throughout, even where those borders might appear arbitrary to modern readers. Heywood's dramatic work was characterised by such fluctuations, to a variety of effects, occasionally mixing verse and prose within one speech (see, for example, 1.1.11 and 4.3.145). Where a verse line overruns, the over-running part of that line has been justified to the right-hand margin and retains the original line number, to distinguish it from a new prose line.

The speech headings have been expanded from their abbreviated form throughout, but are otherwise unchanged unless stated in the Collation.

Glosses in the commentary are supported by the *OED* but it is cited only when either the precise meaning of a word in the text is

INTRODUCTION 31

problematic, or when the *OED* definition offers other contemporary examples of the word or phrase.

Richard Peeke/Pike is called 'Peeke' in his autobiographical pamphlet, but 'Pike' in *Dick of Devonshire*. I refer to 'Peeke' when citing the pamphlet and to 'Pike' when citing the play, in order to be faithful to each text and to enable a clear distinction between the two documents.

NOTES

1 Bullen.
2 Clark, 142; and Boas, as cited in Malone, x.
3 Bedford et al., 142; Long, 146.
4 James and Mary McManaway, the editors of the 1955 Malone Society edition, proposed Robert Davenport, noting extensive similarities between *Dick of Devonshire* and Davenport's *The City Night Cap*, licensed two years previously (Malone, x). James Shirley's name was first put forward in 1891 by F. G. Fleay, who connected *Dick of Devonshire* with Shirley's play *The Brothers*, licensed for performance in November 1626. Fleay, cited in Malone, x. Mark Beeson (137–77) detected John Ford's style in *Dick of Devonshire*'s subplot, citing similarities between the plot of Eleonora and Henrico, and scenes from *The Witch of Edmonton* ascribed to Ford, most notably those between Susan and Frank.
5 Craig. I am indebted to Dr Heather Froelich and Carole Sutton for their help with the statistical modelling for this section. Note that the sample used was relatively small in terms of factor analysis, being n = 120 and 40 variables. Since the time of my writing the introduction, Brett Greatley-Hirsch, Matteo Pangallo, and Rachel White have conducted their own statistical modelling for each of Malone's contenders for *Dick of Devonshire*'s authorship, the results of which also conclude Heywood is the play's likeliest author.
6 The exercise was run separately for each individual playwright.
7 Craig, paragraph 26.
8 Quotations from Peeke's *Three to One* are taken from the copy in the Huntington Library. Caution should be exercised regarding the date of Peeke's return to Fowey. While there is probably some element of truth to the month at least, there is the possibility that a little artistic licence has been applied, emphasising Peeke's Englishness through his return on 23 April, St George's Day.
9 Malone, ix.
10 *Calendar of State Papers Domestic: Charles I, 1625–1626* (London, 1858); *Calendar of State Papers (Venetian): 1623–1625* (London, 1912); *Calendar of State Papers (Venetian): 1625–1626* (London, 1913).
11 Cecil; Grosart; Peeke. Bedford et al. (125–45) offer a detailed and comprehensive analysis of all three accounts.
12 Birch, 104. The ellipsis originates in Birch's transcription.
13 Anon., *A true relation of a brave English strategem practised lately upon a sea-towne in Galizia, (one of the Kingdomes in Spaine) and most valiantly*

32 DICK OF DEVONSHIRE

*and succesfully performed by one English ship alone of 30. tonne, with no more
than 35. men in her. As also, with two other remarkeable accidents betweene
the English and Spaniards, to the glory of our nation* (London: Mercurius
Britannicus, 1626), sig. B2v.

14 Birch, 65.
15 Manning, 114.
16 Grosart, 40.
17 See Frey and Lieblein for a comprehensive study of Heywood's understanding of the tradition of female fasting and self-starvation within
which *A Woman Killed with Kindness* sits.
18 Rowland, 206.
19 Rowland (232) demonstrates that, while editors of *The English Traveller*
have argued to move the composition date back from 1626–27 to 1624,
the evidence for such an argument is tenuous, and 'until and unless new
evidence comes to light, the date of the 1626–27 previously assigned to
the play can and should be accepted'.
20 Lopez, 124.
21 Rowland, 206.
22 British Library MS Egerton 1994, fols. 30–51, Anon., *Dick of Devonshire*.
23 Greg; Bentley.
24 Samuel Chappuzeau, *Le Théatre François* (1674), cited in Peters, 44.
25 Malone, viii.
26 Malone, vii.
27 McManaway, 31.
28 Boswell, 140.
29 For work on playhouse documents, see particularly Stern; Palfrey
and Stern. Gary Taylor's expansive textual analysis of Middleton's *A
Game at Chess* would be difficult to better. See Taylor and Lavagnino.
T. H. Howard-Hill's significant scholarship in this area must also be
acknowledged.
30 The pre-script is, perhaps, more familiarly termed the author's 'foul
papers'. However, I prefer Taylor's terminology of the pre-script, as it
emphasises the functional nature of the manuscript.
31 Long, 146–68.
32 Long, 151.
33 Bedford et al., 142.
34 Contemporary references to Richard Peeke are set out in Appendix 2.
35 Malone, ix; Hoenselaars, 221.
36 *ODNB*.
37 Malone, xii.
38 Munro.
39 Dessen and Thomson.
40 Dustagheer. Heywood would go on to write for the King's Men in
August 1634, when he collaborated with Richard Brome on *The Late
Lancashire Witches*, but in 1626 he had no prior association with that
company.
41 Dustagheer.
42 Ioppolo.
43 Ioppolo, 128.
44 Rowland, 3.

INTRODUCTION 33

45 Thomas Dekker, *The guls horne-booke* (London: Nicholas Okes] for R. S[ergier?], 1609), sig. C2v.

46 James Shirley, *The grateful servant a comedy* (London: B[ernard] A[lsop] and T[homas] F[awcet] for John Grove, 1630), sig. G1r.

47 Marchitello, 242.

48 Stewart, 19–20.

49 Clare, 212.

50 *A proclamation commanding all inhabitants on the sea-coastes, or any ports or sea-townes, to make their speedy repaire unto, and continue at the places of their habitations there, during these times of danger* (London: Bonham Norton and John Bill, 1626).

51 Hammer.

52 Samuel Purchas, *Hakluytus Posthumus or Purchas his pilgrimes. Contayning a history of the world, in sea voyages & lande-travells, by Englishmen & others* (London: W[illiam] Stansby for H. Fetherstone, 1625).

53 Anon., *The voyage of the wandring knight shewing the whole course of mans life, how apt hee is to follow vanitie, and how hard it is for him to attaine to vertue* (London: William Stansby, 1626); Philip Nicholls, *Sir Francis Drake revived calling upon this dull or effeminate age, to folowe his noble steps for golde & silver* (London: Edward Allde for Nicholas Bourne, 1626). Hammer (641) includes a survey of publications relating to Essex.

54 Hammer, 640.

55 Birch, 87.

56 *Upon the English fleete sett forth. Anno. 1625*, Beinecke MS Osborn b.197, p. 226.

57 Cecil, sig C2v; Grosart.

58 Collier, ed., III.i71–2.

59 *A libell of Cales vyage 162* [*sic*], BL MS Harley 6383.

60 Hoenselaars, 219.

61 Grosart, 70.

62 Hoenselaars, 219.

DICK OF DEVONSHIRE

Hector adest secumque Deos in prœlia ducit

Hector adest secumque Deos in prœlia ducit] 'Hector approaches and leads the gods to battle.' This motto also appears on the title page of *The Bloody Banquet*, a play attributed to Thomas Dekker and Thomas Middleton. See Taylor for an analysis of the evidence base for this attribution.

Dramatis Personae

The Duke of Macada
The Duke of Girona
The Duke of Medina   *4 Grandees*
The Marquesse d'Alquevezzes

DON PEDRO GUSMAN   *An ancient Lord*
MANUELL
HENRICO   *Sons of Don Pedro*
DON FERNANDO   *Governor of Cadiz Town*
TENIENTE   *Justicer*
BUSTAMENTE   *Captain of Cadiz Castle*
DICK PIKE   *The Devonshire soldier*
DON JOHN   *A colonel*
BUZZANO   *Servant to Don Pedro Gusman*
ELEONORA   *Daughter to Don Fernando*
CATELINA   *Wife to Don John*

A Gentlewoman
An English Captain
Mr Jewell
Mr Hill
Secretary
Mr Woodrow
A Jailer

TENIENTE, Justicer] A ruler or governor invested with judicial authority.

An English Captain] Thomas Portar, the captain of the *Convertine*, the ship that Dick Pike served on.

Mr Jewell] Master William Jewell. It is not clear from contemporary records whether Jewell was with the *Convertine* or another of the ships in the fleet.

Mr Hill] A Master of the *Convertine* (his forename is not recorded).

Secretary] John Glanville, secretary to the Council of War for the 1625 Cadiz expedition.

Mr Woodrow] A fellow prisoner with Pike. Woodrow is not recorded in contemporary accounts of the 1625 Cadiz expedition.

DICK OF DEVONSHIRE 37

Two Friars
A Guard
English soldiers
Spanish soldiers

Act 1

Scene 1

Enter DON PEDRO GUSMAN, HENRICO *and*
MANUELL, *his sons;* DON FERNANDO *and*
ELEANORA, *his daughter, and* TENIENTE.

Don Pedro. Gentlemen, y'have much honoured me to take
    Such entertainment, but y'are welcome all.
    'Twas my desire to have your company
    At parting. Heaven knows when we shall meet again.
Teniente. You are for France then, too?
Manuell.   I wait on my father.   5
Don Pedro. Henrico?
Don Fernando.   Eleonora.
Teniente. But how chance, Manuell, your younger brother
    Is at the gaol before you? What, no lady to please your
    eye?
Manuell. I am not yet weary of my freedom. May Henrico
    Meet joy in his election; yet I know not   10

The play opens in Cadiz, as Don Pedro Gusman, an ancient nobleman, prepares to travel to France with his son, Manuell. Between them, the characters assembled on stage form the core governance of Cadiz – Gusman, the ruling lord, Don Fernando, the Governor of Cadiz, and Teniente, its Justicer. Their parting, here, leaves the governance of Cadiz vulnerable, and opens the way to the challenges that will be played out in both the main plot and the secondary plot. It is significant that the next time the three characters appear together again is at the end the trial in Act 5, when authority is restored once more.

3–4. *'Twas ... parting*] Your departure now makes me sad, not to have had you stay longer.

5. *wait on*] will accompany.

6. *Henrico?*] Whom, then, are you attending, Henrico? Don Pedro and Manuell are departing for France; Henrico chooses to stay with Eleonora in Cadiz.

7. *is at the gaol*] is nearing the imprisonment of marriage. Said jestingly; with a pun perhaps on *goal.*

10. *election*] choice (of a bride).

38

SC I]   DICK OF DEVONSHIRE   39

one I would sooner choose to call a sister than Eleonora.

Don Pedro. At my return from France all things shall be
    Consummate. In mean time, let your own hearts
    Knit with the strongest tie of love. Be merry
    In mutual embraces, and let your prayers   15
    Fill our departing sails. Our stay will not
    Be long, and the necessity of my affairs
    Unwillingly doth take me from you.

Henrico. [*to Don Pedro*] Though I could wish your stay, my
        duty bids me
    Expect the enjoying of my happiness   20
    Till your return from France. Your blessing.

Eleonora. [*to her father*] How ever Heaven dispose of Eleonora,
    Pray write me in your thoughts, your humblest daughter,
    That shall make it a part of her devotions
    To pray for you.

Don Fernando. [*to Don Pedro*] Well sir, since your design   25
    Pulls you away, may your good angel guard you.

Teniente. The like wish I, Don Pedro.

Don Fernando.   Manuell, I hope
    You will not long breathe out of Spanish air;
    Farewell.

Don Pedro.   My thanks to all. Stay.

              Pieces discharged. Enter BUSTAMENTE.

Don Fernando. The captain of the castle come to interpret   30
    That language to us. What news?

Bustamente.   Such as will
    make all Spain dance in Canary: the Brazil fleet.

---

13. *Consummate*] completed; also implying the consummation of the union between Eleonora and Henrico.

28. *You ... air*] you will not be gone long from Spain, breathing in another land,

29. *Stay.*] Wait a moment; the firing of the cannon announces something you should hear first.

29.1. SD Pieces discharged] Cannons are fired.

31. *That language*] the loud 'speaking' of the cannon.

32. *dance in Canary*] dance a lively early modern court dance (with a glancing reference to the Canary Islands, important in the fleet trade).

the Brazil fleet] One of the treasure fleets of a convoy system operated by Spain to transport exotic goods from the Spanish colonies in the New World back to Spain.

40 DICK OF DEVONSHIRE [ACT I

Don Pedro. Arrived?
Bustamente. Is putting into harbour, and aloud
    Calls for a midwife; she is great with gold 35
    And longs to be delivered.
Don Pedro.   No he Spaniard
    Is not a true rejoicer at the news.
    Be it a good omen to our journey!
Teniente. So we wish all.
Don Pedro. May we, at our return, meet no worse news 40
    Than now at parting. My noble Don Fernando
    And Teniente, once more farewell. My daughter (I hope),
    Eleonora. Henrico. Nay, your good news deserves a
        farewell.
Bustamente. [*to Don Pedro and Manuell*] A soldier's farewell:
    a fast hand and heart. Good fate to both.
                [*Exit* DON PEDRO *and* MANUELL.]
Henrico. Come, Elinor, let them discourse their joys 45
    For the safe fleet. In thee, all my delights embark
    Themselves.
Bustamente.   Tush, let 'em come. Our ships have brought
    With them the news of war.
Don Fernando.   What is that, gentlemen?
Teniente. I am speaking of a fleet of enemies.
Don Fernando. From whence?
Teniente.   From England.
Don Fernando.   A castle in the air. 50
Teniente. Do you not believe it?
Don Fernando.   I heard such a report

---

35. *great*] pregnant.
36–7. *No ... news*] No Spaniard who fails to rejoice at this news can be called a true and loyal subject.
41–2. *My ... hope*] Don Pedro gives his permission and blessing for his daughter, Eleonora, to marry Henrico on Don Pedro's return to Spain.
44. *farewell*] a blessing at the time of my departure.
fast hand] closed fist.
45. *Elinor*] a diminutive of Eleonora.
45–6. *their joys ... fleet*] their hopes for a safe and happy journey.
50. *A castle in the air*] a frivolous speculation. Don Fernando is incredulous about the report of an English fleet approaching.

SC I]　　　　　　DICK OF DEVONSHIRE　　　　　　41

But had no faith in't; a mere Pot gun.
Bustamente. Nay, sir, tis certain there hath been great
　　preparation
　　If our intelligence be true to us;
　　And a mighty navy threatens the sea.　　　　　　55
Don Fernando. What's that to us? How long hath it been a
　　voice
　　They were at sea? I have ventured to discharge the
　　soldiers,
　　Which to keep here in pay upon the rumour
　　Of a great fleet a coming would both pester
　　The town and be unnecessary charge to the King, our
　　master.　　　　　　60
Teniente. But how if they intend us?
Don Fernando.　　　　　　　　　　'Tis not probable.
　　The time of year is past, sir, now, more than
　　The middle of October. Had they meant us,
　　We should have heard their message in loud cannon
　　Before this time.
Bustamente.　　　　I am of that opinion.　　　　　　65
Teniente. But, Don Fernando and Bustamente, call to mind
　　The time hath been when we supposed, too,
　　The season past, they have saluted us
　　With more than friendly bullets, tore the ribs
　　Of our town up, made every house too hot　　　　　　70
　　For the inhabitants, had a spoil of all, spite of our
　　hearts.

---

52. *a mere Pot gun*] Bullen notes this as the early form of 'pop-gun', but
it is also figurative; something noisy or alarming but otherwise insignificant.
Cf. Webster's *The Duchess of Malfi* (1623), 3.3.10, and Congreve's *Old
Batchelour* (1693), 3.1.24.

56–7. *How long ... at sea?*] How long has this threatening navy been
reported to have taken on its journey here?

60. *charge*] expense.

61. *intend us?*] intend to attack us?

67–8. *when ... us*] when we similarly assumed the season of the year too
late to be suitable for an enemy attack, and yet the enemy assaulted us. See
note on lines 72–3 below on the English raiding of Cadiz in 1596.

69. *bullets*] cannon balls.

71. *had a spoil of all*] despoiled us of everything; took all as their prize of
war.

42   DICK OF DEVONSHIRE   [ACT I

Don Fernando. One swallow makes not summer. Because
        once
    Our city was their prize, is't of necessity
    It must be so again?
Bustamente.   Or were the navy
    Greatest (as fame gives out it is the fairest   75
    That ever danced upon these seas), why yet
    Should we suspect for this city?
Don Fernando.   Because we dream so.
Teniente. If you did dream, it may be as near truth.
    I wish the contrary, but know them daring enemies.
Don Fernando. The world, we do acknowledge, cannot boast   80
    More resolution than the English hearts seasoned for
        action.
Teniente. Francisco Bustamente, how is the castle? What
        strength?
Bustamente. A fort impregnable, wanting neither soldiers
        nor munition.
Teniente. Well, look to't.
Don Fernando.   Howe'er that will be necessary, the fort
    Lies in the mouth of danger, and it will become   85
    You to discharge that duty, Bustamente.

---

75. greatest] *Q;* greater *Malone.*

---

72. *One ... summer*] The appearance of one swallow (a migrating song-
bird) does not necessarily mean that summer has arrived. Proverbial wisdom,
urging caution against jumping to conclusions.
   72–3. *Because ... prize*] The English successfully raided Cadiz in 1596.
The 1625 expedition was intended to mirror the earlier celebrated raid, but
failed. See introduction, pp. 24–6.
   74–5. *Or were ... Greatest*] Even if this navy were the mightiest on the high
seas.
   75. *fame*] reputation.
   fairest] handsomest.
   77. *suspect for*] fear for the safety of.
   83. *wanting*] lacking.
   84. *look to't*] make sure the fort is impregnable, as you assert.
   Howe'er ... necessary] No matter how well these necessary precautions are
carried out.
   85. *become*] suit, befit.
   86. *discharge*] carry out.

sc 2]   DICK OF DEVONSHIRE   43

Bustamente. With my best care.
Teniente. I wish all well, and that you had not yet
    Discharged your companies, Don Fernando.
Don Fernando. Come, come, put off your jealousy, drink
    down the remembrance;   90
    We forget our fleet's arrival. Send your fears away.
    Nothing but wine and mirth should crown this day.
                            Exeunt.

SCENE 2

Enter two Devonshire Merchants, as being in Jerez.

1 Merchant. Hear you the news?
2 Merchant.   Yes, that an English fleet
    Is making up to Cadiz.
1 Merchant.   Our Jerez merchants,
    Though few of us be here, shall soundly pay
    To the furnishing of this navy.
2 Merchant.   Nay,
    I assure you our ships will be fast bound   5
    By Spanish charms not to get hence in haste.

---

0. SD Jerez] *this ed.; Sherryes, Q.*   2. Jerez] *this ed.; Sherryes, Q.*

---

89. *discharged*] dismissed.
90. *jealousy*] anxieties.
91. *We ... arrival*] We are not taking into consideration the fact that our own fleet is at hand,

SD Jerez] William Long suggests that this stage direction is unusual because it specifies the occupation of the merchants as 'sherry merchants'. However, it makes more sense that the reference is to the merchants' location in the Spanish town of Jerez, in the province of Cadiz. The likeliness of this interpretation is substantiated by line 11's 'all the Dons in Jerez'. The location here makes more sense than the commodity. Of course, this does not preclude the merchants from being traders in sherry, for which the town was renowned.
2. *Our Jerez merchants*] We merchants from Devonshire, trading here in Jerez.
3. *pay*] be taxed as foreigners.
5–6. *will be ... haste*] will be compelled by the Spanish fleet not to leave Jerez any time soon.

44   DICK OF DEVONSHIRE   [ACT I

1 Merchant.   The devil already
     Is furling up the sails. Would all the sacks
     Which we have bought for England were in Devonshire
     Turned to small beer, so we were but in Tavistock
     To see it drawn out, were it ne'er so thin!   10
     I'd drink a health to all the Dons in Jerez
     And cry a pox upon 'em.
2 Merchant. That word heard by any lousy Spanish picardo
     Were worth our two necks. I'll not curse my diegoes,
     But wish with all my heart that a fair wind   15
     May with great bellies, bless our English sails,
     Both out and in; and that the whole fleet may
     Be at home delivered of no worse a conquest
     Than the last noble voyage made to this city,
     Though all the wines and merchandise I have here   20
     Were i'th' sea's bottom.
1 Merchant.   Truth, so would I, mine.
2 Merchant. I ne'er could tell yet from what root this huge
     Large spreading tree of hate from Spain to us,
     From us again to Spain, took the first growth.
1 Merchant. No? Then I'll tell you. Let us season our sorrow   25
     With this discourse.
2 Merchant.   With all my heart I long for't.
1 Merchant. You shall not lose your longing. Then, sir, know
     The hate a Spaniard bears an Englishman

---

7. *is ... sails*] is readying the Spanish fleet to take action against us.
would] I wish that.

7–10. *Would ... thin*] I could wish that all the containers we have acquired for our wine business were in Devonshire now, being used for cheap English beer, and I wish that we were there too, in the Devonshire town of Tavistock, to see the alcoholic contents being drawn out of their containers for customers, no matter how thin that beer might be.

12. *And ... 'em*] and curse them all.

13. *picardo*] scoundrel, rogue.

14. *Were ... necks*] would warrant a hanging for both of us.

15–21. *that ... bottom*] that a fair wind might fill the sails of our English ships on both their outward journeys and their return, so that the whole fleet might have at least as safe a voyage as that of the English expedition to Cadiz in 1596; I could wish for this even at the risk of losing everything to misadventure at sea.

23–4. *hate ... Spain*] mutual hatred between England and Spain.

24. *took ... growth*] first began.

SC 2] DICK OF DEVONSHIRE 45

Nor natural is, nor ancient; but as sparks,
Flying from a flint by beating, beget flames, 30
Matter being near to feed and nurse the fire,
So, from a tinder at the first kindled,
Grew this heartburning twixt these two great nations.

2 Merchant. As how, pray?

1 Merchant.   Hear me: any Englishman
That can but read our chronicles can tell 35
That many of our kings and noblest princes
Have fetched their best and royalest wives from Spain,
The very last of all binding both kingdoms
Within one golden ring of love and peace
By the marriage of Queen Mary with that little man, 40
But mighty monarch, Phillip, son and heir
To Charles the Emperor.

2 Merchant.   You say right.

1 Merchant.   Religion,
Having but one face, then both here and there,
Both nations seemed as one. Concord, commerce,
And sweet community were chains of pearl 45
About the necks of either. But when England
Threw off the yoke of Rome, Spain flew from her.

---

29. *Nor natural*] neither natural.

32.] Bullen suggests it would be an improvement to read 'enkindled', or
'kindled at the first', but the former would exceed the iambic pentameter
and the latter would interrupt the rhythmic assonance of the line.

38. *The very last*] of all the most recent of royal marriages between Spain
and England.

40–1. *By ... Phillip*] By the marriage of Queen Mary I of England to King
Philip II of Spain, in 1554. Philip II was not tall.

42. *Charles*] Charles V, Hapsburg Emperor of the Holy Roman Empire,
1519–56, and King of Spain, 1516–56.

42–3. *Religion ... there*] The Catholic Church still at that time being one
church of western Europe, though in fact by 1554 the Reformation was well
underway, and England under Henry VIII had broken with the Papacy. This
event is referred to below in lines 46–7, but the First Merchant misleads
when he suggests that England's throwing off the yoke of Rome took place
after Queen Mary I's marriage to Philip II of Spain.

46–7. *when England threw off the yoke of Rome*] The Act of Supremacy
(1558) established Elizabeth I as the supreme head of the Church of England
and rejected the authority of the Pope.

46   DICK OF DEVONSHIRE   [ACT I

Spain was no more a sister nor a neighbour,
But a sworn enemy. All this did but bring
Dry sticks to kindle fire; now see it burn.   50
2 Merchant. And warm my knowledge and experience by't.
1 Merchant. Spain's anger never blew hot coals indeed
   'Til in Queen Elizabeth's reign, when (may I call him
     so?)
   That glory of his country, and Spain's terror,
   That wonder of the land and the seas' minion,   55
   Drake, of eternal memory, harrowed th'Indies.
2 Merchant. The King of Spain's West Indies?
1 Merchant.   Yes. When his hands -
   Nombre de Dios, Cartagena, Hispaniola,
   With Cuba and the rest of those fair sisters -
   The mermaids of those seas – whose golden strings   60
   Gave him his sweetest music – when these were ravished
   By Drake and his brave ginges, when these red apples
   Were gathered and brought hither to be pared,
   Then the Castilian lion began to roar.
2 Merchant. Had he not cause, being vexed so?
1 Merchant.   When our ships   65
   Carried such fire drakes in them, that the huge
   Spanish galleasses, galleons, hulks and carracks,
   Being great with gold, in labour with some fright,

---

51. *And ... by't*] The Second Merchant's meaning here is unclear.
Following the First Merchant's order to 'now see it [the kindled fire of
Anglo-Spanish relations] burn' in line 50 above, the most probable meaning
is that the Second Merchant wants to learn more (to be warmed by the
flames) about the history of the tension between England and Spain (the
fire), to inform his current experience. If the First Merchant was already in
full knowledge of the relationship between the two countries, the Second
Merchant's further exposition would be dramatically clumsy.

56. *Drake ... th'Indies*] the eternally famous Sir Francis Drake raided
Spanish ports and shipping in the West Indies, 1585–86.

57. *his hands*] King Philip's ships.

61–3. *when these ... pared*] when these delectable fruits of the Spanish fleet
were plucked and harvested by the English.

62. *ginges*] followers.

64. *the Castilian lion*] Philip of Castile, Philip II.

66. *fire drakes*] dragons, i.e. cannon. Also a pun on Sir Francis Drake.

68. *great*] pregnant, i.e. heavily laden. The pregnancy metaphor is continued in 'in labour', later in the line.

SC 2]   DICK OF DEVONSHIRE   47

    Were all delivered of fine red cheeked children
    At Plymouth, Portsmouth, and other English havens,   70
    And only by men midwives, had not Spain reason
    To cry out, 'oh *Diables Ingleses*'?
2 Merchant. It had not spoke such Spanish else.
1 Merchant. When we did set our feet even on their mines,
    And brought their golden fagots thence, their ingots,   75
    And silver wedges; when each ship of ours
    Was able to spread sails of silk, the tacklings
    Of twisted gold; when every mariner
    At his arrival here had his deep pockets
    Crammed full of pistolets; when the poorest ship-boy   80
    Might on the Thames make ducks and drakes with
        pieces
    Of eight, fetched out of Spain, these were the bellows
    Which blew the Spanish bonfires of revenge.
    These were the times in which they called our nation
    Borachios, Lutherans, and Furias del Inferno.   85
2 Merchant. Would we might now give them the self-same
        cause
    To call us so.
1 Merchant.   The very name of Drake
    Was a bugbear to fright children. Nurses stilled

---

    69. *delivered of*] brought to childbirth with.

red cheeked] Gold was often spoken of as reddish in hue.

    71. *And ... midwives*] and with no one assisting at the birth except the men of the English fleet.

    72. Diables Ingleses] English devils.

    73. *It had ... else*] There was nothing else that the poor discomfited Spanish could say.

    75. *golden fagots*] bundles of gold.

    80. *pistolets*] Spanish gold coins.

    81. *duck and drakes*] a game of spinning flat stones or shells along the surface of calm water; a metaphor for reckless squandering. The hyperbole here is that even erstwhile penniless ship-boys will have so many good coins that they will be able to throw some away carelessly for fun.

    85. *Borachios*] drunkards (literally 'wine-bags').

Lutherans] As Protestants, Lutherans bore a name that became a swear word to Spanish Catholics.

Furias del Inferno] devils of hell.

    86. *self-same*] very same.

    88. *bugbear*] an imaginary being invoked by nurses to frighten children.

48 DICK OF DEVONSHIRE [ACT I

Their little Spanish ninnies when they cried.
'Hush, the Drake comes!'

2 Merchant. All this must needs beget 90
Their mortal hate to us.

1 Merchant. It did. Yet then,
We loved them beyond measure.

2 Merchant. Why?

1 Merchant. Why, did not Spain fetch gold from the West
Indies
For us to spend here merrily? She planted vines;
We eat the grapes. She played the Spanish pavine 95
Under our windows; we in our beds lay laughing
To hear such minstrelsy.

2 Merchant. How, then, turned the winds?
Why did this beauteous face of love in us
Put on so black a visor of hate to them?

1 Merchant. Oh, sir, do but look back to eighty-eight. 100
That Spanish glass shall tell you; show each wrinkle.
England, that year, was but a bit picked out
To be laid on their king's trencher. Who were their
cooks?
Marry, sir, his Grandees, and great Dons of Spain.
A navy was provided; a royal fleet, 105
Infinite, for the bravery of admirals,
Vice admiral, generals, colonels and commanders,
Soldiers, and all the warlike furniture,
Cost or experience or man's wit, could muster
For such a main design.

2 Merchant. Stay. Eighty-eight? 110
Thirty-eight years ago. Much about then
Came I into the world. Well, sir, this fleet–

---

89. *ninnies*] children (alteration of Spanish *niño*).
90. *must needs*] must necessarily.
95. *pavine*] Music accompanying a stately court dance. See also Dekker's
Blurt Master Constable (1602) (*OED* 1a).
100. *eighty-eight*] 1588, when Philip II's Spanish Armada attempted
(unsuccessfully) to invade England.
101. *glass*] mirror, reflecting the truth of history.
103. *their King's trencher*] Philip II's dinner plate.
109. *cost*] that cost.

| SC 2] | DICK OF DEVONSHIRE | 49 |

1 Merchant. Which made the sea-fish wonder what new
    kingdom
  Was building over theirs; beat down the billows
  Before them to get thither. 'Twas such a monster   115
  In body, such a wonder in the eyes,
  And such a thunder in the ears of Christendom,
  That the Pope's Holiness would needs be godfather
  To this most mighty big-limbed child, and call it
  Th'invincible Armada.
2 Merchant.   That's to say   120
  A fleet of ships not to be overcome
  By any power of man.
1 Merchant.   These were the whales.
  These were the huge leviathans of the sea
  Which roaring came, with wide and dreadful jaws,
  To swallow up our kingdom, ships, and nation.   125
  The fame of this Armada flew, with terror
  Riding on Envy's wing. The preparation
  Was waited on with wonder, and the approach
  Showed the grim face of horror. Yet 'gainst all these
  Our country and our courages were armed.   130
2 Merchant. St. George for England!
1 Merchant.   And 'St. George', we cried,
  Albeit, we heard, the Spanish Inquisition
  Was aboard every ship, with torture, torments,
  Whips strung with wire, and knives to cut our throats.
  But from the armèd winds, an host brake forth   135
  Which tore their ships, and saved ours. Thus I have
    read
  Two stories to you: one, why Spain hates us,
  T'other, why we love not them.
2 Merchant.   Oh, sir, I thank you.
                              Exeunt.

---

117. *such a*] Bullen speculates that 'the repetition of the words "such a"
is probably a clerical error: the Alexandrine is clumsy'. However, the trilogy
fits into the Alexandrine of the rest of the speech, suggesting that its repetition was deliberate.

50   DICK OF DEVONSHIRE   [ACT I

SCENE 3

Enter TENIENTE, DON JOHN, *and* HENRICO.

Teniente. I ever feared some ill fate pointed at
    This city.
Don John.   Makes the fleet this way?
Henrico. [calling]   Buzzano?
Teniente. I did dream every night of't, and the ravens
    With their unlucky throats never leave croaking
    Some danger to us all.
Henrico.   Where's Buzzano? Villain!   5
Don John. Be not discomforted.
Teniente.   Don Fernando too
    Hath cut our strengths off, taken away our swords
    Should save our throats. I did prejudicate
    Too rashly of the English. Now we may
    Yield up the town.

Enter BUZZANO.

             Sirrah, get you up   10
    To th'highest turret, that looks three leagues into the sea,
    And tell us what you can discover there.
Buzzano. Why, I can tell you ere I go.
Henrico. What?
Buzzano. Why, there are fishes and ships too in the sea. They   15
    were made for that purpose.
Teniente. The fellow dotes. Climb quickly, sirrah, and tell us
    Whether any bend to this place. There's a fleet
    Abroad; scud, rascal!
Henrico. Villain, away, and cast your eyes into the sea.   20
Buzzano. I'll be hanged first. Some wiser than some. Mine
    eyes into the sea? I see no reason for't.

---

    8. *Should*] that should.
    17. *dotes*] speaks foolishly.
    18. *bend*] to approach.
    19. *scud*] make haste.
    21. *Some wiser than some*] Some people think they are wiser than us plain
folks. Buzzano interprets casting one's eyes into the sea literally and sees it
as a frivolous idea.

SC 3] DICK OF DEVONSHIRE 51

Teniente. Why stayest thou? This slave is without sense.
    Get up and see, and report the truth.
Buzzano. That's another matter. I will overlook you all   25
    presently.

                       [*Exit* BUZZANO.]

Don John. What were I best to do? I do not like these navies.
Henrico. 'Tis past question, if they were kenned this way,
    That they intend to make another meal of this city.
Teniente. The first was but a breakfast. They have shrewd
                               stomachs.   30
    Oh, for a lusty storm to bury all
    their hopes in the waves now. One good swelling gust
    would break their ribs in pieces.

              Enter BUZZANO *above.*

Don John. No witches abroad?
Buzzano.   I see. I see. I see.
All. What?
Buzzano. Nay, I cannot tell what yet.   35
    Something it is. I think it be a town.
Henrico. Some island in the sea?
Buzzano.   It swims on the water.
Don John. 'Tis the fleet. Come they this way?
Buzzano.   Yes, th'are ships.
    I know 'em by their foul linen. Now I see
    Them plainly. They come, they come, they come!   40
Henrico. How far off?
Teniente.   Speak, sirrah.
Buzzano. If you would peace, I might hear what they say.
    The wind serves to bring every word they speak.
    They make towards, yes, towards this city.
    A great fleet. Stay, stay! Look to your selves, Dons.   45

---

31. all.] *Q; all Malone (subst.).*

  23. *stayest thou?*] are you just standing there?
slave] wretch.
  28. *kenned*] known to be coming.
  30. *They ... stomachs*] They are spoiling for a fight.
  31. *lusty*] powerful. Teniente is presumably recalling what happened to the
Armada in 1588.
  42. *peace*] hold your peace; be quiet.

52 DICK OF DEVONSHIRE [ACT I

They spit fire already, and have hung up a thousand
    flags
of defiance. They are at the fort. The castle, at the
    castle!
Would I were pelted to death with oranges and lemons!
Teniente. Here comes Don Fernando.

        Enter FERNANDO *with* ELEONORA.

                        What news?
Fernando. Assured danger, gentlemen, for all our men   50
    Already are in a palsy and do fly
    They know not whither. They are English.
    The city's almost desperate.
Teniente.   Don John, come with me
    and help to encourage the remaining soldiers.
Fernando. New supply shall quickly cheer your hearts.
    Henrico?
Henrico.   Sir?   55
Fernando. In this confusion, when a thousand fears
    Present themselves, and danger with full face
    Looks on the general town, let me lock up
    This treasure in your arms. And, for you have
    At least an equal interest with me   60
    In Eleonora, in your father's house
    She may hope more security being of strength,
    For this storm cannot last; but in your love
    She hath a stronger guard.
Henrico.   This act of confidence
    Binds me for ever to Fernando. [*To Eleonora*] Come,   65
    Half of my soul, for we two must not be
    In life divided. Though the city lie
    At mercy of the enemy, yet from
    Don Pedro Gusman's house not all mankind
    Shall take thee from me.   70

---

62. security] *Q;* security; *Malone.*

    46–7. *flags of defiance*] red flags displayed as a sign of readiness for battle
(also known as 'bloody flags'). Although in widespread use prior to this date,
the flag of defiance did not appear in English naval instructions until 1647.
    59. *This treasure*] i.e. Eleonora.
    for] since.

SC 3]   DICK OF DEVONSHIRE   53

                  Enter BUZZANO *and* Spaniards, *flying.*

Buzzano. They come! They come! They come!
Fernando. Committing this, my jewel, to your trust,
    I must unto my charge. My blessing.
Eleonora. Oh, do not leave me sir, for without you
    What safety can I have? You are my father.   75
    Pray, stay you with me.
Fernando.   Oh, my girl, I cannot,
    Dare not, be so unfaithful to the trust
    His Majesty put me in, though I would stay.
Eleonora. I fear if you go hence, all will not long be well.
Henrico. Distrust you me, Eleonora?
Eleonora.   No, indeed.   80
    You ever had with me th'opinion
    Of a most noble gentleman.
Fernando.   What then?
Eleonora. I know not what besides my fear, and that
    Begs I may share your fortune, since you may
    Not take up such safety here as I have.   85
Fernando. Come, you are to blame. This Heaven that now
        looks on us
    With rugged brow may quickly smile again,
    And then I shall revisit my Eleonora. So, farewell.
                              Exit FERNANDO.
Henrico. Till when, with greater care than were the dragons
    Supposed to watch the golden apples growing   90
    In the Hesperides, shall Henrico wait
    On his best loved. Oh, my Eleonora,
    I would to Heaven there were no war but here
    To shoot love darts! Each smile from this fair eye

---

73. *My blessing*] Take my blessing with you.
81–2. *You ... gentleman*] I have always regarded you as a most noble
gentleman.
83–5. *and that ... have*] my fears prompt me to beg that I may stay with
you, since you might not be able to enjoy the safety you would have if you
stayed here.
89–91. *the dragons ... the Hesperides*] In Greek mythology, the daughters
of Hesperus guarded, with the aid of a watchful dragon, the garden in which
golden apples grew in the Isles of the Blest, at the western extremity of the
earth.

54   DICK OF DEVONSHIRE   [ACT I

May take an army prisoners. Let me give   95
My life up here unto these lips, and yet
I shall, by th'sweetness of a kiss, take back
The same again. Oh, thou, in whom alone
Virtue hath perfect figure, hide not day
In such a cloud. What fear hath entered here?   100
My life is twisted on a thread with thine.
Were't not defenced, there could nothing come
To make this cheek look pale, which at your eye
Will not fall dead before you.

Enter BUZZANO.

Sirrah, let all your care and duty be   105
Employed to cheer this lady. [*To Eleonora*] Pray, be
                                                              merry.
Buzzano. Oh, sir, yonder's such doings!
Henrico. Hell on your bawling! Not a syllable to affright her,
    or I shall tune your instrument there.
Buzzano. [*to himself*] He'll break the head of my instrument.   110
    [*To Henrico*] Why sir, women are not afraid to hear of
    doings.
Henrico. Still jarring?
Buzzano. When the whole town is altogether by th'ears, you
    might give me leave to jar a little myself. I have done, sir.   115
Henrico. Put on thy merriest face, Buzzano.
Buzzano. I have but one face, but I can make a great many.
Henrico. My best Eleonora, I shall soon return.
    In the meantime, be owner of this house;
    The possessor. All danger, sweet, shall dwell   120
    Far off. I'll but enquire the state of things in the city
    And fly back to thee with love's wings.
                                                        Exit HENRICO.

102–4. *defenced ... you*] I would kill any unprotected thing that would
cause the colour to leave your cheek (i.e. through distress or pain), if you
signal that I should do so. There might be a link to the mythical beast, the
basilisk, which struck dead anything that met its gaze. This would foreshadow
Don Pedro's metaphor of Eleonora's letter as 'stuck all with Basilisks' eyes'
in 3.3.13, below.
    113. *jarring*] arguing.
    114. *by th'ears*] quarrelling.

| SC 3] | DICK OF DEVONSHIRE | 55 |

Eleonora. I prithee, call him back.
Buzzano. [*calling*]   Signor Henrico!

[HENRICO *returns*].

She has something more to say to you.
Henrico. To me, sweetest?
Eleonora.   Henrico, do you love me?   125
Henrico. By this fair hand.
Eleonora.   And will you leave me too?
Henrico. Not for the wealth of Spain.
Eleonora. Since I must be your prisoner, let me have
    My keeper's company; for I am afraid
    Some enemy, in your absence, like a wolf   130
    May seize on me. I know not whether more
    I e'er shall see my father. Do not you
    Ravish yourself from me, for at the worst
    We may die here Henrico, and I had rather
    Fall in your eye than in your absence be   135
    Dishonoured. If the destinies have not
    Spun out our longer threads, let's die together.
Henrico. Oh, do not wrack my soul with these sad accents!
    Am I Henrico? There's not any place
    Can promise such security as this   140
    To Eleonora. Do not talk of dying.
    Our best days are to come. Put on thy quiet,
    And be above the reach of a misfortune.
    I'll presently wait on thee; by this kiss. [*He kisses her.*]
Buzzano. Would I might keep your oath! So please you,
                                    Lady,   145

---

123. SD HENRICO *returns*] *this ed.; redit, Q.*   144. thee;] *Malone (conj.);
possibly* thee, *Q.*

---

126. *By ... hand*] I swear, by the lovely hand of her whom I love; or, by
his own hand. A common form of oath.
    leave me too?] i.e. leave me, despite your loving me?
129. *My keeper's company*] the company of you, my guardian and
protector.
135. *in your eye*] in your presence.
140. *Can*] that can.
142. *Put on thy quiet*] Be still.
144. *I'll ... kiss*] I will constantly attend to your needs; I promise this, by
this kiss.

56 DICK OF DEVONSHIRE [ACT I

Buzzano will swear too.
Henrico. What?
Buzzano. That you'll be there and here again presently.
Henrico. Attend her, sirrah.
Buzzano. If you must needs go,
Pray, sir, keep yourself out of gunshot.
Henrico. Mind you your charge. 150
Buzzano. You shall hear a good report of my piece, I warrant
you. Take heed you be not sent to Heaven with a powder!
A company of hotshots are abroad, I can tell you.
Eleonora. If you will go, may your success be fair.
Henrico. Farewell. Heaven cannot choose but hear that
prayer. 155

Exit.

Buzzano. Now, what please you, madam? That I shall amble,
trot, or walk?
Eleonora. Any pace.
Buzzano. Yet if you would refer it to me, I'd use none of them.
Eleonora. What wouldst do? 160
Buzzano. Why I would gallop or run, for I think long till I be
at home, in our castle of comfort. If it please you, I'll lead
you a hand gallop, madam, in the plain ground, trot up
hill with you, and rack downwards.
Eleonora. Talk not of racks, prithee. The times present too 165
many.
Buzzano. Ride me as you will, then. I am used both to curb
and snaffle.

---

147. *That ... presently*] Buzzano comically misinterprets what Henrico has
said to mean that he will be absent (on military business) only briefly and
will quickly return to safety.

148. *Attend her, sirrah*] Wait on Eleonora while I am gone, you rascal.

150. *charge*] responsibility; assignment.

151. *my piece*] my doing what I have been told to do.

152. *with a powder*] by being fired at.

159. *refer it to me*] allow me to choose.

164. *rack*] go at a horse's gait. Eleonora, in her response, plays on the
meaning of an instrument of torture.

167. *curb*] A chain or strap passing under the lower jaw of a horse, and
fastened to the upper ends of the branches of the bit; used chiefly for check-
ing an unruly horse.

168. *snaffle*] A simple form of bridle-bit, having less restraining power
than one provided with a curb.

SC 3]   DICK OF DEVONSHIRE   57

Eleonora. I prithee tell me, Buzzano – so I hear thy master call
  thee.   170
Buzzano. He may call me at his pleasure, forsooth.
Eleonora. Dost thou know the nature of the English?
Buzzano. Both men and women. I travelled thither with an
  ambassador. For the men, I'll not miss you a hair of their
  condition; and for the women, I know 'em as well as if I   175
  had been in their bellies.
Eleonora. Are they not cruel?
Buzzano. As tigers when they set on't. No mercy, unless we
  ask them forgiveness.
Eleonora. That's somewhat yet.   180
Buzzano. But not to you; that's only to men. For let the
  women fall down afore 'em never so often, they'll rather
  fall upon them. Nay, some of them are so spiteful, they'll
  break their own backs before they'll let 'em rise again.
Eleonora. Fool, I mean not your way.   185
Buzzano. Keep your own way, madam; I mean the plain way.
Eleonora. Are they not unmerciful in their natures to such as
  are in their power? Their enemies, as we may be?
Buzzano. Their enemies as we may be in their power? I had
  rather be cramm'd into a cannon, and shot against their   190
  ships, than you should prove a witch and tell true now.
  The Tartar is not half so grim; not a Turk would use us
  so like Jews as they will. If it come to that once, that they
  take the town, you shall see Spanish Dons' heads cried
  up and down as they do our oranges and lemons; and the   195

---

174. *For*] As for. Also in line 175, below.
  a hair] a slightest detail.
182–4. *fall down ... rise again*] Buzzano finds material for bawdy by-play
in this conversation. Eleonora refutes that suggestion in her reply in line 186.
  185. *Fool*] a) simpleton; b) stage fool, a recognisable type.
  192. *Tartar*] A native inhabitant of the region of central Asia extending
eastward from the Caspian Sea, and formerly known as Independent and
Chinese Tartary. First known in the West as applied to the mingled host of
Mongols, Tartars, Turks, etc., which under the leadership of Jenghiz Khan
(1202–27) overran and devastated much of Asia and Eastern Europe (*OED*
A1).
  194–5. *cried ... down*] loudly announced in the streets, as food or other
items might be announced by vendors.

58   DICK OF DEVONSHIRE   [ACT I

women's heads shall off too. Not a maidenhead of gold
shall scape 'em.

Eleonora. It is no valour to use tyranny
    Upon the conquered. They have been reported
    A noble nation; and when last the pride   200
    Of this city adorned their victory, by command
    Of their brave general, no outrage ever
    The soldiers durst commit upon our persons.
    Though all our wealth ran in full streams upon them,
    Our honours were preserved, or fame belies them.   205

Buzzano. [*Aside*] No matter what fame says, perhaps I know
    more than she does.

[*To Eleonora*] And yet, now you talk of valour, they are not
    comparable to us.

Eleonora. How?   210

Buzzano. Why, valour is but the courage of a man. Courage
    is, as they say, the spirit of a man; and the spirit of a man
    is the greatness, as we call it, of his stomach. Now 'tis
    well known to the whole world they feed better and eat
    more than we. Ergo, we have better stomachs than they.   215
    But, see. We have talked ourselves at home already, and
    the point is open; will't please you enter? Or shall I enter
    before you? I am your man, madam.

Eleonora. You know the way best. Whilst abroad they are
    At fight, twixt hope and fear at home, I war.   220

                                                        Exeunt.

---

196. *maidenhead of gold*] A representation of the head and shoulders of a
young woman in full face, couped below the breasts, with her hair loose and
often dishevelled (usually wreathed with a garland and crowned with an
eastern crown), used as a heraldic charge, as a maker's mark on silver or
goldware, etc. Also a common bawdy jest referring to a woman's virginity.
Compare *Romeo and Juliet*, 1.1.25–6: 'The heads of the maids, or the
maidenheads?'

206. *fame*] reputation; rumour.

215. *stomachs*] a) appetites; b) courage.

216. *talked ourselves at home*] talked the whole time we have been walking
towards our house.

217. *point*] i.e. the home; the house.

219–20. *Whilst ... fight*] While the Spanish and English armies engage in
fighting outside the city.

Act 2

SCENE I

*Alarum; as the soft music begins, a peal of ordnance
goes off; then cornets sound a battle; which ended,
enter* CAPTAIN, Master of a Ship [JEWELL],
I SOLDIER, DICK PIKE, *with muskets.*

Captain. Fought bravely, countrymen. Honour all this while
    Sat in a throne of smoke with sparkling eyes
    Looking upon your courages, and admiring
    Your resolutions, and now rewards your sweat
    With victory. The castle groans at heart;   5
    Her strongest ribs are bruised with battering cannons,
    And she hath ta'en into her bowels fire enough to melt
               her.
Jewell. My Lord came bravely up to her, and showed a
               spirit
    that commands danger. His honourable example
    gave us new hearts.   10
I Soldier. Faith give the Spaniards their due, they entertained
    us handsomely with hot meat. 'Twas no cold welcome.
Pike. But I would not willingly swallow their plums; they
    would rise shrewdly in a man's stomach.
Captain. At the first shot, when the Convertine came in,   15
    Three men were killed.
Jewell.   At the second, four was't not?
Captain. At the third, two more.
    One salutation came so close that with the very wind
    My hands have almost lost the sense of feeling.

  0.1 SD peal of ordnance] A loud discharge of guns or cannon fire.
  0.2 SD *Master of a Ship*] The Master on stage in this scene is Jewell, rather
than Hill, as is made clear at line 20.
  11–12. *they entertained ... meat*] the Spaniards fought back with relish.
  15. *Convertine*] The name of the ship that Richard Peeke served on.

59

60   DICK OF DEVONSHIRE   [ACT 2

Jewell, thou mad'st thy musket spit fire bravely.   20
Jewell. And my Devonshire blade, honest Dick Pike,
     Spared not his sugar pellets among my Spaniards.
Captain. He did like a soldier. As he that charged his musket
     told me, in this service he hath discharged seventy bullets.
Pike. I did my part, sir, and wished I had been able to have   25
     laid 'em on thicker. But I have lined somebody's guts,
     much good do 'em with it. Some of them have wished
     well to me.
Captain. Art hurt?
Jewell. Where?   30
Pike. Nowhere. One of my flanks itches a little. If a piece of
     lead have crept in to hide itself cowardly, I am not much
     in debt for't.
Captain. Let my surgeons search it.
Pike. Search a pudding for plums. Let my flesh alone. Perhaps   35
     it wants soldering. Shall we to't again, I have half a score
     pills yet for my Spaniards; better than purging comfits.

Enter 2 SOLDIER.

Captain. What news?
2 Soldier. The fort is yielded.
Pike. They have been speechless a good while. I thought   40
     they'd yield up the ghost shortly.
2. Soldier. But on condition to march away with flying colours,
     Which was granted.
Captain. What's become of the captain of the fort?
2 Soldier. Don Francisco Bustamente is carried aboard our   45
     general's ship where he had a soldier-like welcome. But
     he and all his company are put over to Port Real, upon
     the mainland, because they should not succour the city.
Captain. Unless he will swim to th'island. And how fares the
     Convertine?   50

---

22. *sugar pellets*] bullets.
31–3. *If a piece ... for't*] if I have been shot, it is not causing me much
inconvenience.
37. *pills*] bullets.
39. *is yielded*] has surrendered.
41. *yield up the ghost*] surrender. Compare Matt. 27.50: 'Jesus, when he
had cried again with a loud voice, yielded up the ghost.'
48. *because ... the city*] because they should not be able to help the city.

SC I]   DICK OF DEVONSHIRE   61

2 Soldier. Her shrouds are torn to pieces, and her tacklings to
   rags.
Captain. No matter; she carries the more honour.
2 Soldier. Five hundred bullets stick in her sides.
Pike. 'Tis well they scaped her heart. Lying all the fight little   55
   more than pistol shot from 'em, her starboard still to the
   fort, and at the least two hundred muskets playing upon
   her. I wished heartily some of our London roaring boys
   had been in the heat of't.
2 Soldier. Wouldst have 'em twice burnt?   60
Pike. They should have found a difference betwixt the smoke
   of tobacco and of a musket; another manner of noise,
   then damn me and refuse me, which they vomit daily. It
   might have done some of 'em good, for by that means
   they might have prayed heartily once in their lives.   65
Captain. The Whitehall men did good service.
Jewell. Who? The Colliers?
1 Soldier. Four thousand bullets, their ordinance, and the
   Hollanders discharged upon the castle.
Captain. 'Twas well done of all sides, bullies.   70
   But since our forces are landed, let it be
   Your care to look well to the ships. And honest Dick
   of Devonshire, be not too careless of your hurts;
   he means to fight again that provides for
   his recovery soonest. Hold thee, here is something   75
   to pay the surgeon and to wash the wound withall.
Pike. My noble captain, I'll have care of my own and drink
   your health with it.
Jewell. Thou deservest more than common encouragement.
   Prithee remember me too.   *Exeunt Captain and Master.*   80

---

55. SH *Pike*] *Q; Pike written in the margin after Cap. had been cancelled.*

---

51. *shrouds*] a set of ropes, usually in pairs, leading from the head of a
mast and serving to relieve the latter of lateral strain; they form part of the
standing rigging of a ship.
   tacklings] the rigging of a ship.
   58. *roaring boys*] boys given to or characterised by noisy, riotous, or
drunken behaviour (*OED* B1).
   70. *bullies*] term of friendly admiration.
   73–5. *be not ... soonest*] Do not underplay your injuries. The quicker you
recover, the sooner you can fight again.

62   DICK OF DEVONSHIRE   [ACT 2

Pike. Why, now am I sorry I have no more hurt gentlemen;
    but I took it as earnest to receive more, if occasion be. I
    have but a barrel to bestow among my Dons. While that
    lasts, let 'em come and welcome. The drink shall be
    spiced to their hands. Their complexions are black; they   85
    shall want no balls to wash their faces. If any do light in
    their bodies, they may chance be scoured all over.
2 Soldier. We may hap to be in the suds ourselves.
Pike. There will be charges saved then. For my part, I am but
    one, and there will be shots enough.   90
2 Soldier. More by a score, then I hope we'll be paid these
    two days.
Pike. Talk not of paying; here's more than a month comes to.
    Well, if our service be done, and there be any other liquor
    to be got, we'll drink no salt water as long as this lasts.   95
2 Soldier. Come, let's have a dish to our countrymen, and let's
    remember Tavistock.
Pike. Godamercy for that, boy. A match, a match.

                                             Exeunt.

                        SCENE 2

        Enter HENRICO, *his sword drawn, and* ELEONORA.

Henrico. Yet the city is safe enough. Fear not, Eleonora.
    The bullets make no noise here. If the town
    Should yield her strength up to th'invader, thou

85–7. *they shall ... all over*] Cannonballs will cleanse the English fleet of
the Spanish enemy. Here, cannonballs are equated with the soap-scented
balls that were becoming increasingly popular in seventeenth-century
Europe. Compare Gervase Markham's instructions for making washing balls
in *The English Housewife* (1615): 'To make very good washing balls, take
storax of both kinds, Benjamin, Calamus Aromaticus, Labdanum of each a
like; and bray them to powder with cloves and arras; then beat them all with
a sufficient quantity of soap till it be stiff, then with your hand you shall
work it like paste, and make round balls thereof' (sig. L3v).

88. *We may hap to be in the suds ourselves*] We might be hit by cannon fire
ourselves. This anticipates the colloquialism 'to be in hot water', which came
into common usage in the eighteenth century.

97. *Tavistock*] Richard Peeke's home town, a small town on the edge of
Dartmoor, south-west England. Coincidentally, it was also the home town
of Sir Francis Drake.

DICK OF DEVONSHIRE

Art locked up like a spirit in a crystal.
Not an enchanted castle, held up by 5
Strong charm, is half so safe. This house, though now
It carry not the figure and fair shape
Which the first workman gave it, eating time
Having devoured the face of 't, is within
A sanctuary, and hath so much cunning 10
Couched in the body, not a labyrinth
Is so full of meanders.

Eleonora.   Sir, your presence
Confirms me in opinion of my safety;
Not of my life so much, for that's a thing
I owe to nature, and should one day be 15
A weary of it. Like to inns we take
Our houses up, having but here a place
Of lodging, not of dwelling. But of honour
You give me my assurance, for in such
A time of thick confusions, I much feared 20
That might be hazarded. And who knows what
The soldier, that hath no law but that
Of cruelty and rapine, when like a bird
Of prey, his talons are possessed of one
So weak as I am?

Henrico.   He that durst offend 25
Thee with a syllable, or but fright that blood
Out of thy cheeks to seek another place,
Not daring to be seen there where it now
Is, of itself sufficient to ravish
A mortal that with just eyes can look on it, 30
Had better be a devil. But a hair,
The poorest part of thee, and in this excellent
Because 'tis thine, should any dare to ravish
From these his soft companions, which the wind
Would be forever proud to play withall, 35
H'had better dig his mother's coffin up
And with his teeth eat what the worms have left.

---

4. *like a spirit in a crystal*] Chapter 12 of Reginald Scot's *Discoverie of
Witchcraft* (1584) is entitled 'How to enclose a spirit in a christall stone'.

14–18. *Not of … dwelling*] We borrow our lives from nature, and dwell in
our bodies only as long as nature intends.

64   DICK OF DEVONSHIRE   [ACT 2

Eleonora. I know you will defend me.
Henrico.   Will defend thee?
    Have I a life? A soul that in thy service
    I would not wish expired? I do but borrow   40
    Myself from thee.
Eleonora.   Rather you put to interest,
    And for that principal you have credited
    To Eleonora, her heart is paid back
    As the just usury.
Henrico.   You undo me, sweet,
    With too much love; if e'er I marry thee,   45
    I fear thou'lt kill me.
Eleonra.   How?
Henrico. With tendering me too much, my Eleonora.
    For in my conscience thou'lt extremely love me,
    And extremes often kill.
Eleonora.   There can be no extreme of love, sir.
Henrico. Yes, but there may, and some say jealousy   50
    Runs from the sea; a rivulet but deducted
    From the main Channel.
Eleonora.   This is a new language.
Henrico. Have you not heard men have been killed with joy?
    Our grief doth but contract the heart, and gladness
    Dilate the same, and so too much of either   55
    Is hot i'th' fourth degree.
Eleonora.   Sir, your discourse
    Is stuff of several pieces, and knits not
    With that you used but now. If we can practise
    A virtuous love, there's no hurt to exceed in't.
    What do you, sir?
Henrico.   Look on thee.   60
Eleonora. Why do you eye me so? This is not usual.

40–1. *I do but borrow myself from thee*] Henrico echoes Eleonora's analogy.
See note to 2.2.14–18, above.

41–4. *Rather you … just usury*] Rather, you (Henrico) lend yourself to me
(Eleonora), and I pay you back with interest, with my love.

49. *There can be no extreme of love*] Cf. *The Two Gentlemen of Verona* (1592),
2.7.70, 'instances of infinite of love'.

57. *stuff*] woven material. Cf. Middleton and Webster's *Any Thing for Quiet
Life* (1632) (*OED* 5b).

SC 2] DICK OF DEVONSHIRE 65

Are you well?
Henrico.   Well? Never better.
Eleonora. Pray Heaven, it bode me no unhappiness.
  How doth my father?
Henrico.   He's very well, too; fear not.
Eleonora. Still, I read in your eyes–
Henrico.   What, babies? Pretty one,   65
  Thy own face, naught else. I received that way
  All this beauty into my heart, and 'tis
  Perhaps come back to look out at the window.
  Come, I'll wink again. It shall not trouble you.
  Hence my traitorous thoughts.
Eleonora.   Indeed, you are not well.   70
Henrico. Indeed I am not; all's not well within me.
  Why should I be a villain? Eleonora,
  Do not look on me; turn those eyes away.
  They would betray thee to thy sorrow or
  Let me, by parting, carry along with me   75
  That which to know undoes thee.
Eleonora.   Are you not hurt?
Henrico. Yes.
Eleonora. Good Heaven defend, I have a sovereign balm.
                            Exit ELEONORA.
Henrico. Vanish you ugly shapes, and with her presence
  Quit your sharp stings. Into what monstrous creature   80
  Feel I myself a growing? Yet I cannot
  Force back the stream, it comes so fast upon me.
  I cannot.

                  Enter ELEONORA.

Eleonora.   Here, good Henrico, let me see your wound.
Henrico. No, I am well again, thanks my best love.
  Come, let us walk and talk. I had a fancy–   85

---

  65. *Still … one*] Bullen notes that to 'look babies in the eyes' was a
common expression for peering amorously into the eyes.
  66–8. *I … window*] Your (Eleonora's) beauty filled my (Henrico's) heart
so much that it overflowed, and now reflects back to you through my eyes.
Henrico plays on the idea of the eyes as the window to the soul.
  69. *I'll wink again*] I will close my eyes so the look is gone.
  78. *sovereign*] efficacious.

66 DICK OF DEVONSHIRE [ACT 2

But 'tis no matter. [*Calling*] Buzzano?

Enter BUZZANO.

Buzzano. Did you call?
Henrico. Yes. The balm, here.
Buzzano. What shall I do with it?
Henrico. Lay it up safe. 'Tis good for a green wound,
    But mine's a black one. And d'you hear, sirrah,
    Draw up the bridge; give entrance unto none.   90
Buzzano. All my fellows are abroad sir; there's nobody at
    home but I.
Henrico. No matter, let none enter. Were my father
    Brought with a whirlwind back, he finds all shut
    'Til I have done.   95
Buzzano. [*To Henrico*] Well, sir. [*To Eleonora*] Madam, all this
    is that you should not be afraid. You now see what a kind
    man he is? He will suffer none to enter but himself.
                       [*Exit* BUZZANO.]
Eleonora. If all this proceed out of your care of me, how much
    am I bound to acknowledge you? Sir, me thinks you mind   100
    me not.
Henrico. Yes, I do nothing else but think of thee, and of my
    father too, Don Pedro.
Eleonora. Ha? I hope he's well?
Henrico. I wish he were returned, my Eleonora, for both our   105
    sakes.
Eleonora. The same wish I, sir.
Henrico. That then our joys which now, like flowers nipped

88–9. *'Tis good ... black one*] The balm that Eleonora has provided will treat a wound related to the green humour, but not to the black one that afflicts me. The classical theory of the constitution of four humours – blood, phlegm, yellow bile, and black bile – was still current in the early seventeenth century, and medical treatment was targeted specifically at the humour that was believed to be unbalanced.

93–5. *Were my ... have done*] Do not let anybody into the house until I say otherwise, not even my father, should he return home early.

96–8. *Madam ... but himself*] Buzzano unwittingly puns on entering the castle and Henrico entering Eleonora through the act of sexual intercourse.

102–3. *and of my father too, Don Pedro*] See the note to 1.1.6, above. Henrico has promised his father he will wait on Eleonora, in her father's absence.

DICK OF DEVONSHIRE

With frost, hang down the head as if the stalks
Could not sustain the tops, they droop too much. 110
At his return, th'art mine.

Eleonora.   I am yours now
In holiest contract.

Henrico.   That's the ground we build on.
Faith, since already the foundation's laid,
Let's work upon't. Y'are mine, you say, already;
Mine by all terms of law, and nothing wanting 115
But the possession. Let's not then expect
Th'uncertainty of a return from France
But be all one immediately.

Eleonora.   I understand you not.

Henrico. Since y'are a tree reserved for me, what now
Should hinder me from climbing? All your apples 120
I know are ripe already. 'Tis not stealth;
I shall rob nobody.

Eleonora.   You'll not be a devil?

Henrico. No, I will but play the man with you. Why, you
                         know 'tis nothing.

Eleonora. Will you enforce mine honour? Oh, Henrico,
Where have you lost your goodness? Sure you cannot 125
be so ignoble, if you think me worthy to be your wife
at least, to turn Eleonora into a whore?

Henrico. Pish, some hungry landlords would have rent before
The quarter day; I do no more. By fair means,
Yield up your fort. The tenement is mine own 130
And I must dwell in't.

Eleonora.   My fears pointed wrong.
You are no enemy, no wolf; it was
A villain I distrusted. Oh, make me not
Find in your presence that destruction
My thoughts were so affrighted with. 135

Henrico. We shall have such ado now?

---

129. *quarter day*] each of the four days fixed by custom as marking off the quarters of the year, on which some tenancies begin and end, the payment of rent and other quarterly charges fall due, and on which quarterly meetings were formerly often held.

130. *Yield up your fort*] Let down your defences. This idea of fortification is echoed by Eleonora in line 137, below.

68 DICK OF DEVONSHIRE [ACT 2

Eleonora. Your father's house will prove no castle to me,
 If you at home do wound me. 'Twas an angel,
 Spoke in you lately, not my cheek should be
 Made pale with fear. Lay not a lasting blush   140
 On my white name. No hair should perish here,
 Was voiced even now. Oh let not a black deed,
 And by my sworn preserver, be my death.
 My ever living death. Henrico, call
 To mind your holy vows. Think on our parents,   145
 Ourselves, our honest names. Do not kill all
 With such a murdering piece. You are not long
 T'expect, with the consent of men and angels,
 That, which to take now from me, will be loss;
 A loss of Heaven to thee. Oh, do not pawn it   150
 For a poor minute's sin.
Henrico. If't be a work, madam, of so short time,
 Pray let me beg a minute's privacy.
 'Twill be soon done.
Eleonora.   Yes, but the horror of
 So foul a deed shall never; there's laid up   155
 Eternity of wrath in Hell for lust.
 Oh, 'tis the devil's exercise. Henrico,
 You are a man; a man whom I have laid up
 Nearest my heart. In you, 'twill be a sin
 To threaten Heaven, and dare that Justice throw   160
 Down thunder at you. Come, I know you do
 But try my virtue; whether I be proof
 Against another's battery. For these tears—
Henrico. Nay, then I see you needs will try my strength.

137–8. *Your father's ... wound me*] Your father's house will offer me no
protection if I am wounded by somebody who is already in the house.

138–43. *'Twas an angel ... be my death*] The juxtaposition of black and
white, immorality and reference, is a recurring theme in the play. Cf. 'Such
a reverend habit / Should not give harbour to so black a falsehood' (5.1.441–2).

141. *white*] pure.

150. *pawn*] The Eleonora/Henrico plot is reminiscent of the subplot of
Middleton's *A Game at Chess* (1625), in which the White Queen's Pawn is
raped by the Black Bishop's Pawn.

155. *shall never*] never be done.

161–3. *Come ... battery*] I know that you are testing my honour and fidelity, to see if I would resist anyone else, should he approach me.

SC 2] DICK OF DEVONSHIRE 69

My blood's on fire; I boil with expectation   165
To meet the pleasure, and I will. [*He forces her in.*]
Eleonora.   Help! Help!

[*Enter* BUZZANO.]

Buzzano. Help? What nightingale was that? Did one cry out
for help? There's no Christian soul in the house but they
two, and my self, and 'twas not mine; I know by the
smallness of the voice. 'Twas some woman cried out, and   170
therefore can be none but my young lady. It was she as
sure as I am hungry; he's with her. But why, having one
man, did she cry out for more? Oh, our Spanish ovens
are not heated with one bavin. Well, I must say nothing.
My young cock has been treading. I'll tread softly and   175
see if I can hear what they do. But, see.

Enter HENRICO *and* ELEONORA, *loose haired,
and weeping.*

Henrico. What do you look after?
Buzzano. Why, sir, I look after a voice that appeared to me
even now, crying help; a very small one.
Henrico. If what thou seest or heard'st be ever muttered by
thee,   180
Though in thy sleep, villain, I'll pistol thee.
Buzzano. Hum, it will not be safe to dream of a knave shortly.
Are you so good at a gun? If you use this too often, your
birding piece will scarce carry a yard level.
Henrico. [*to Eleonora*] Come, dress your hair up, and be wise   185
at last. No more, I have done.
Buzzano. [*Aside*] So I think in my conscience, he hath done
with her.
Henrico. If you can be so simple to proclaim it, I can be
impudent.   190

---

166. SD *Enter* BUZZANO] *Bullen (subst.).*   181. sleep,] *Malone (conj.);
perhaps* sleep; *Q.*

---

174. *bavin*] a bundle of quick-burning brushwood or light underwood
used in bakers' ovens.

175. *young cock has been treading*] The cockerel (i.e. Henrico) has been
copulating with the hen (i.e. Eleonora).

70 DICK OF DEVONSHIRE [ACT 2

Eleonora. Yet dar'st thou live? And do I live to see
  Myself the shame of women? Have I not
  Wept tears enough to drown me? Then let fire
  Enthrone itself within me and beget
  Prodigious comets that, with flaming hairs,   195
  May threaten danger to thee.
Henrico.   Nay, nay, nay,
  If you be so hot I'll leave you; like wine that's burnt,
  You must be set light by, and then you'll come to a
      temper.   *Exit.*
Eleonora. Oh help me out of Hell.
Buzzano. [*Aside*] Sh'has been at Barley-break. [*To Eleonora*]   200
  Madam, I must say nothing. There is a pistol and so forth.
  But if you have occasion to use me, try me. If I do not
  prove an honester man to you than my master, would my
  codpiece point were broke. I know what I know, and yet
  I'll tell no tales. But ever I come to speak once, I say   205
  nothing.
Eleonora. Oh, that I could not breathe! How can I have
  A joy in life, whose honour's in the grave?
                                                    Exeunt.

SCENE 3

Enter PIKE, *with his sword in his hand, a cloak
        on his arm.*

Pike. The freshness of this air does well after the saltiness of
  the sea. A pleasant country, too, to look upon, and would

---

195. *flaming hairs*] the tail of the comet.

197. *wine that's burnt*] The precise early sense is doubtful, but is believed
to be that from which part of the alcohol has been removed by burning
(*OED* 5).

200. *Barley-break*] An old country game, varying in different regions,
originally played by six persons (three of each sex) in couples; one couple,
being left in a middle den termed 'hell', had to catch the others, who were
allowed to separate or 'break' when hard pressed, and thus to change part-
ners, but had, when caught, to take their turn as catchers. Bullen notes that
the term was also often used in a wanton sense.

201. *There is a pistol and so forth*] i.e. the pistol that Henrico threatened
to shoot Buzzano with in line 174, above.

SC 3]   DICK OF DEVONSHIRE   71

serve well to live upon if a man had it, and knew how to
place it out of this hot climate. I would I had a matter,
or a manor indeed, of a thousand acres of these wood-   5
lands, and room to set it in Devonshire. I would compare
with any prince between Tavistock and Paradise for an
orchard. But I could wish I were not alone here in this
conceit, dreaming of golden apples, lest they prove bitter
fruit. Whither are our land soldiers straggled true? I   10
would fain set eye on some of them. I'll venture a little
further; Devonshire Dick was never afraid yet.

Enter three Soldiers

How now, my hearts. Upon a retreat so soon?
1 Soldier. I, to the ships. We have our loads here of the best
    merchandise we can find in this quarter.   15
2 Soldier. Will you taste a lemon? Excellent good to cool you.
Pike. They are goodly ones; where got you them?
3 Soldier. A little above here, in an orchard, where we left some
    of our company.
Pike. But may one go safe, without danger?   20
1 Soldier. As safely as ever you gathered nuts in England. The
    Spaniards are all fled.
2 Soldier. Not so much as the leg of a Spaniard left to squall
    at their own apple trees.
                                        Exeunt Soldiers.
Pike. I'll have a pull at these pomme-citrons for my noble   25
    captain; and if I had a porter's basket full of 'em, I would
    count them no burden in requittal of some part of the
    love he hath shown me.
                                                Exit.

---

22. fled] *Q;* fled. *Malone (subst.).*

8–10. *I could wish ... fruit*] I wish I was not alone, in case I am ambushed
while I daydream.

26. *porter's basket*] Cf. *The Porter and the Three Ladies of Baghdad*, one of
the stories in *One Thousand and One Nights* (otherwise known as *The Arabian
Nights*). Although not printed in English until 1706, stories were circulating
orally in folk tales from the tenth century.

72   DICK OF DEVONSHIRE   [ACT 2

SCENE 4

Enter three other Soldiers.

1 Soldier. They cannot be far before us I am sure.

2 Soldier. But for the hedge, we might descry them within two
musket shot.

3 Soldier. Pray God the enemy be not within one musket shot
of us, behind these hedges; for I am sure I saw an har-   5
quebuse whip o'er the way before us but even now.

Three or four shots discharged. Two Soldiers slain,
the other falls on his belly.

Oh, oh.   *Enter* PIKE.

Pike. Are you bouncing? I'll no further. Sure, these can be no
crow keepers nor bird scarers from the fruit? What rascals
were my countrymen to tell me there was no danger?   10
Alas, what's here? Three of our soldiers slain? Dead, shot
through the very bowels. So, is this quite dead too? Poor
wretches, you have paid for your capon sauce.

3 Soldier. Oh, oh.

Pike. [*Aside*] There's some life in it yet. [*To Soldier*] What   15
cheer? How is't, my heart of gold? Speak man, if thou
canst. Look this way. I promise thee 'tis an honest man
and a true Englishman that speaks to thee. Thou look'st
away as if thou didst not trust me. I prithee speak to me
anything; I'll take thy word and thank thee too. [*Aside*]   20
Alas, I fear he's past it; he strives, and cannot speak. 'Tis
good to shift this ground; they may be charging more
hidden villainy while I stand prating here. He breathes
still. [*To Soldier*] Come, thou shalt not stay behind for
want of legs or shoulders to bear thee. If there be surgery   25
in our ships to recover the use of thy tongue, thou mayst
one day acknowledge a man and a Christian, in honest

5–6. *harquebuse*] early type of portable gun, varying in size from a small
cannon to a musket.

8. *bouncing*] the making of loud, explosive noise, as of guns or cannons.

13. *you have paid for your capon sauce*] i.e. with your lives.

22. *shift this ground*] leave this place.

24–5. *Come ... thee*] You will not have to stay behind just because you
cannot walk and there is nobody to carry you.

SC 4] DICK OF DEVONSHIRE 73

Dick of Devonshire. Come along. [*Aside*] Nay, now I fear
my honesty is betrayed. A horseman proudly mounted
makes towards me, and 'tis a Don that thinks himself as   30
brave as St. Jaques himself. What shall I do? There is no
starting; I must stand th'encounter. [*To Soldier*] Lie still
awhile and pray if thou canst, while I do my best to save
my own and the little breath thou hast left. [*Aside*] But I
am in that prevented too; his breath's quite gone already,   35
[*To Soldier*] and all the Christian duty I have now left for
thee is to close thy eyes with a short prayer. Mayst thou
be in Heaven, Amen. [*Aside*] Now Don Diego, and Don
Thunderbolt, or Don Devil, I defy thee.

> Enter DON JOHN, *armed*. PIKE *draws and wraps*
> *his cloak about his arm.*

Don John. Oh *viliaco. Diabloe. Anglese.*   40
Pike. A pox upon thee, Hispaniola.

> *They fight.*

Nay, if you be no better in the rear then in the van, I shall
make no doubt to vanquish, and vanquash you too,
before we part, my doughty Don Diego.

> *He hath him down and disarms him.*

Don John. Mercy Englishman! Oh, spare my life. *Pardonne moi* 45
   je vous pre.
Pike. And take your goods? Is that your meaning, Don? It
   shall be so. Your horse and weapons I will take, but no

---

32. *starting*] running.
40. viliaco] a vile or contemptible person.
42. van] shortening of 'vanguard', meaning forefront.
43. *vanquash*] to smash.
44. *doughty*] honourable.
45–6. Pardonne moi je vous pre] It is unclear why Don John appeals to
Dick Pike in French rather than Spanish. It is possible that he hopes to fool
the Englishman into thinking he is a Frenchman and, therefore, not a threat,
as Anglo-French relations were favourable following Charles I's marriage to
Queen Henrietta Maria in May 1625. However, this remains problematic
because Don John has already addressed Dick in Spanish at line 40. It is
possible that the author's fluency in Spanish was limited, so French was used
interchangeably.

74　　DICK OF DEVONSHIRE　　[ACT 2

pilferage. I am no pocketeer, no diver into slops; yet you
may please to empty them yourself, good Don, in recom-　50
pense of the sweet life I give you. You understand me well.
This coin may pass in England. What is your Donship
called, I pray?

Don John. Don John, a knight of Spain.

Pike. A knight of Spain? And I a Squire of Tavistock. Well,　55
Don John, I am a little in haste, and am unmannerly
constrained to leave your Castilian on foot. While my
Devonshire worship shall teach your Spanish jennett an
English gallop, *adios, signior.*

Enter twelve Musketeers.

Oh, what a tide of fortune's spite am I now to swim　60
through? Bear up yet, jovial heart, and while thou knowest
Heaven's mercy, do not start. Once more, let me embrace
you, *signior.*

1 Musketeer. I say he is an Englishman. Let's shoot him.

2 Musketeer. I say the other is a Spaniard, and Don John, and　65
we dare not shoot the one for fear of killing th'other.

Don John. Oh hold, and spare us both, for we are friends.

1 Musketeer. But by your leave, we will part your embraces,
so disarm, disarm.

Don John. I thank you, countrymen. I hope you'll trust my　70
honour with my arms?

1 Musketeer. Yes, take them signior, but you will yield the
Englishman our prisoner?

Don John. Yes, with a villain's mark.

He wounds him.

1 Musketeer. A villain's mark indeed. Wound a disarmed　75
soldier?

Don John. He triumphed in the odds he had of me,
And he shall know that from the Spanish race
Revenge, though ne'er so bloody, is not base.

---

49. *pocketeer*] pickpocket.

62. *start*] flinch.

70–1. *I hope … arms*] I hope you will trust me enough to return my
weapon to me (i.e. after Dick took it from him at line 44).

79. *base*] of a low or inferior quality or standard.

SC 5] DICK OF DEVONSHIRE 75

Away with him; a prisoner into th'city. 80
Pike. Where you please; although your law's more merciless
than seas.

Exeunt.

SCENE 5

Enter DON FERNANDO, *the* TENIENTE, *with
attendants;* BUSTAMENTE *brought in with a Guard.*

Fernando. Francisco Bustamente, late captain of the castle,
Stand forth, accused of treason 'gainst his Majesty.
Bustamente. It is a language I not understand,
And but that, by the rule of loyalty
Unto my king and country, I am made 5
Attendant to the law, and in this honoured
Presence, the Governor and Teniente,
Under whose jurisdiction I hold place,
I would not bear nor hear it.
Fernando. I'd be glad
You could as easily acquit yourself 10
Of guilt, as stand up in your own defence.
But Bustamente, when it doth appear
To law and reason, on which law is grounded,
Your great offence in daring to betray
The Spanish honour unto infamy, 15
In yielding up the fort on such slight cause,
You can no less than yield yourself most guilty.
Bustamente. Far be it from your thought, my honoured Lord,
To wrest the hazardous fortune of the war
Into the bloodier censure of the law. 20
Was it my fault that in the first assault
Our canoniers were slain? Whereby our strength,
Our main offensive strength, was quite defeated,
And our defensive part so much enfeebled

---

3. *language*] accusation.
3–9. *It is … hear it*] I do not recognise the accusation, and if I were not
loyal to my country and to its legal system, I would not allow the accusation
to be levelled against me.
12–17. *But … guilty*] You surrendered the fort to the English unnecessar-
ily, and so you must also surrender yourself to a guilty plea.

76 DICK OF DEVONSHIRE [ACT 2

That possibility to subsist was lost, 25
Or by resistance to preserve one life?
While there was spark of hope, I did maintain
The fight with fiery resolution and
(Give me leave to speak it) like a soldier.
Teniente. To my seeming, your resolution was forwarder 30
To yield than to repel; you had else stood longer out.
Bustamente. We stood the loss of most of our best men
And of our musketeers, no less than fifty
Fell by the adverse shot, whose bodies with their arms
Were cast by my directions down a well 35
Because their arms should neither arm our foes
Nor of our loss the sight give them encouragement.
Fernando. That policy pleads no excuse. You yet
Had men enough, had they been soldiers,
Fit for a leader's justification. 40
And do not we know that six score at least
Of those base picaros, with which you stuffed
The fort to feed not fight, unworthy of
The name of Spaniards, much less of soldiers,
At once ran all away like sheep together, 45
Having but o'er the walls descried th'approach
Of th'enemy? Some of the fear-spurred villains
Were overta'en by slaughter in their flight.
Others were taken, and are sure to find
Our laws as sharp as either sword or bullet. 50
For your part, Bustamente, for that you have
Done, heretofore, more for your country's love,
You shall not doubt of honourable trial
Which in the court of war shall be determined,
At Jerez, whitherward you instantly 55

30–1. *your resolution ... repel*] You were more inclined to surrender than
to fight.

34. *arms*] weapons.

35. *directions*] instructions.

38. *policy*] course of action.

40. *justification*] the showing or maintaining in court of sufficient reason
for having committed the act to be answered for; a circumstance affording
grounds for, or offered as, such a defence.

48. *overta'en by slaughter*] killed.

54. *court of war*] court-martial (*OED* 13b).

SC 5]   DICK OF DEVONSHIRE   77

Shall with a guard be sent. See't done. Away.
Bustamente. The best of my desire is to obey.
                                        Exit with a Guard.

        Enter DON JOHN, PIKE *(with his face wounded),*
                    a guard of muskets.

Fernando. Whence is that soldier?
1 Soldier.   Of England.
Don John.   Or of Hell.
1 Soldier. It was our chance to come unto the rescue
    Of this renowned knight, Don John,   60
    Who was his prisoner as he now is ours;
    Some few more of his mates we shot and slew
    That were (out of their English liquorishness)
    Bold to rob orchards of forbidden fruit.
2 Soldier. It was a fine ambition; they would have thought   65
    Themselves as famous as their countryman
    That put a girdle round about the world,
    Could they have said at their return to England,
    Unto their sons, 'Look boys, this fruit your father
    With his adventurous hands in Spain did gather.'   70
Fernando. 'Tis a goodly fellow.
1 Soldier. Had you not better have gone home without lemons,
    to eat capons with your friends, than to stay here without
    capons, to taste lemons with us that you call enemies.
Pike. I could better fast with a noble enemy than feast with   75
    unworthy friends.
Fernando. How came he by these wounds?
Pike. Not by noble enemies. This on my face
    By this proud man, yet not more proud than base;
    For when my hands were in a manner bound,   80
    I having given him life, he gave this wound.

---

57. SD *wounded),*] *this ed.; wounded,)* Q.

---

    58. *that soldier*] i.e. Dick Pike.
    67. *a girdle round about the world*] contextually, a reference to Drake's
circumnavigation of the world, 1577–80, during which he ransacked several
Spanish territories. However, as Bullen notes, this was a common turn of
phrase. See *A Midsummer Night's Dream* (1595), 2.1.178–9, 'I'll put a girdle
round about the earth / In forty minutes'.

78   DICK OF DEVONSHIRE   [ACT 2

Fernando. 'Twas unadvised.
Teniente.   The more unmanly done;
    And though, Don John, by law y'are not accused,
    He being a common enemy, yet being a man
    You in humanity are not excused.   85
Don John. It was my fury and thirst of revenge.
Fernando. Reason and manhood had become you better.
    Your honour's wounded deeper than his flesh,
    Yet we must quit your person, and commit
    The Englishman to prison.   90
Teniente. To prison with him, but let best care be taken
    For the best surgeons, that his wounds be looked to.
Pike. Your care is noble, and I yield best thanks;
    And 'tis but need, I tell your signiors,
    For I have one hurt more than you have seen,   95
    As basely given, and by a baser person.
    A Fleming, seeing me led a prisoner,
    Cried, 'whither do you lead that English dog?
    Kill, kill him', cried he, 'he's no Christian';
    And ran me in the body with his halbert   100
    At least four inches deep.
Don Fernando. Poor man; I pity thee, but to the prison with
    him.
Teniente. And let him be carefully looked to.

                                Exeunt omnes.

Act 3

SCENE 1

Enter CAPTAIN, HILL, SECRETARY, and JEWELL.

Captain. Our general yet showed himself right noble in offering ransom for poor captive Pike.
Secretary. So largely too as he did, Captain.
Captain. If any reasonable price would have been accepted, it had been given, Mr. Secretary, I assure you.   5
Jewell. I can testify that at our return, in our general's name, and my own, I made the large offer to the Teniente, who will by no means render him. Sure they hold him for some great noble purchase.
Secretary. A Baronet at least; one of the lusty blood, Captain?   10
Captain. Or perhaps, Mr. Secretary, some remarkable Commonwealth's man; a politician in government.
Secretary. 'Twere a weak state-body that could not spare such members. Alas, poor Pike, I think thy pate holds no more policy than a pollax.   15
Hill. Who is more expert in any quality than he that hath it at his fingers' ends? And if he have more policy in his brains than dirt under his nails, I'll ne'er give two groats for a calf's head. But without all question, he hath done some excellent piece of villainy among the diegos, or else   20

---

20. else] *Bullen (subst.);* e< *Q.*

---

10. *lusty blood*] See *King John* (1597), 2.1.470: 'What cannoneer begot this lusty blood?'

13. *state-body*] an allusion to the body politic, a metaphor in which a nation is regarded as a corporate entity, with the monarch as the head (*OED* 1.).

14. *pate*] head.

15. *policy*] political strategy; political cunning.

pollax] poleaxe; originally a weapon for use in close combat, existing in various forms but generally having a head consisting of an axe blade or hammer-head, balanced at the rear by a pointed fluke.

80 DICK OF DEVONSHIRE [ACT 3

they take him for a fatter sheep to kill than he is.

Captain. Well, gentlemen, we all can but condole the loss of
him; and though all that we all come hither for be not
worth him, yet we must be content to leave him. The
fleet is ready, the wind fair, and we must expect him no   25
longer.

Hill. He was a true Devonshire blade.

Secretary. My countryman, sir. Therefore would I have given
the price of a hundred of the best toledoes rather than
hear the miss of him at home complained by his wife and   30
children.

Jewell. Your tenderness becomes you sir, but not the time,
which wafts us hence to shun a greater danger. *Exeunt.*

Scene 2

Enter Pike *in shackles, nightcap, plasters on his face;*
a Jailer.

Pike. The fleet is gone, and I have now no hope of liberty, yet
I am well refreshed in the care hath been taken for my
cure; but was ever English horse thus Spanish bitted and
bossed?

Jailer. Sir, the care of your keeper, by whom this ease hath   5
been procured, requires remuneration.

Pike. Here's for you, my friend.

Jailer. I assure you the best surgeons this part of Spain affords,
through my care taken of you, and you may thank me.

Pike. What an arrogant rascal's this? Sir, I thought my thanks   10
herein had chiefly appertained to the humanity of the
Governor; and that your especial care had been in providing these necessary shackles to keep me from running

---

25. fair] *Malone (subst.);* fai< *Q.*

---

21. *fatter sheep*] more important people.

23. *all that we all come hither*] for i.e. treasure from the treasure fleet.

27. *Devonshire blade*] local attribute.

28. *My countryman*] John Glanville, secretary to the Council of War, was
also from Tavistock, Devon.

29. *toledoes*] swords or sword blades, of the sort made in Toledo; playing
upon Hill's 'Devonshire blade' remark in 3.1.27.

[SC 2]   DICK OF DEVONSHIRE   81

into further danger. These I took to be the strong bonds
of your friendship.   15

Jailer. Sir, I hope they fit you as well as if they had been made
for you; and I am so much your servant that I do wish
'em stronger for your sake.

Pike. 'Tis overwell as it is sir.

Jailer. You are most courteous.   [*Exit* JAILER.]   20

Pike. A precious rogue. If the jailers be so pregnant, what is
the hangman true? By the time my misery hath brought
me to climb to his acquaintance, I shall find a friend to
the last gasp.

> *Enter* CATELINA *and* JAILER.

What's here? A lady? Are the women so cruel here to   25
insult our captive wretches?

Catelina. Is this the English prisoner?

Jailer. Yes, madam.

Catelina. Trust me, a goodly person.

Pike. She eyes me wistly. Sure she comes not to instruct   30
herself in the art of painting by the patterns of my face?

Catelina. Sir, shall I speak with you?

Pike. Yes, Lady, so you will not mock me.

Catelina. Indeed I cannot, but must needs acknowledge
myself beholden to you.   35

Pike. This I must bear; I will do so, and call't my sweet
affliction.

Catelina. Will you hear me sir? I am the Lady—

Pike. Yes, I do hear you say you are the lady; but let me tell
you, madam, that ladies, though they should have tender-   40
est sense of honour, and all virtuous goodness, and so
resemble goddesses, as well in soul as feature, do often
prove dissemblers, and in their seemly breasts bear
cruelty and mischief. If you be one of those, oh, be con-

---

21. *pregnant*] easily influenced. See also *Twelfth Night* (1616) (*OED* 2c).

30. *wistly*] intently.

35. *beholden*] indebted. Catelina is indebted to Pike for saving her
husband.

42. *feature*] physical appearance.

43. *dissemblers*] one who conceals their real purposes under a false appearance; one who practises duplicity; a deceiver, hypocrite (*OED*).

82   DICK OF DEVONSHIRE   [ACT 3

verted. Return from whence you came and know 'tis   45
irreligious, nay devilish, to tread and triumph over misery.
Catelina. How well he speaks! Yet in the sense betraying
    A sense distracted; sure his captivity,
    His wounds, and hard entreaty make him frantic?
    Pray, hear me, sir, and in two words I'll tell you   50
    Enough to win belief. I am the Lady
    Of the Knight vanquished by you, Don John.
Pike. Y'have said enough indeed. Pity of Heaven,
    What new invented cruelty is this?
    Was't not enough that by his ruthless baseness   55
    I had these wounds inflicted, but I must
    Be tortured with his wife's unjust rejoicings?
    'Twas well his politic fear, which durst not come
    To glory in his handiwork himself,
    Could send your priviledged Ladyship.   60
Catelina. Indeed you much mistake me. As I live,
    As I hope mercy, and for after life,
    I come for nothing but to offer thanks
    Unto your goodness, by whose manly temper
    My lord and husband reassumed his life;   65
    And ask your Christian pardon for the wrong
    Which, by your suffering, now pleads him guilty.
    Good sir, let no mistrust of my just purpose
    Cross your affection. Did you know my love
    To honour and to honest actions, you   70
    Would not then reject my gratulations.
    And since that deeds do best declare our meaning,
    I pray accept of this: this money, and these clothes; and
                              my request
    Unto your keeper for best meats and wines,
    That are agreeable to your health and taste.   75
    [*To Jailer*] And, honest friend, thou knowst and darest,
                                    I hope,
    Believe me, I will see thee paid for all.

---

62. life;] *Malone (conj.); perhaps* life, *Q.*

---

  48. *distracted*] having, or showing, great mental disturbance or perplexity.
  58. *politic*] shrewd. Cf. Middleton's *A Game at Chess* (1625), 5.1.34:
'Yonder's my game, which, like a politic chessner, I must not seem to see.'
  67. *now pleads him guilty*] of which he is guilty.
  72. *deeds do best declare our meaning*] actions speak louder than words.

SC 2] DICK OF DEVONSHIRE 83

Jailer. Yes, my good Lady. [*To Pike*] 'Loe you sir, you see still
    how my care provides your good. You may suppose the
    Governor's humanity takes care for you in this too.   80
Pike. [*To Catelina*] Excellent Lady, I do now believe
    Virtue and women are grown friends again.

Enter DON JOHN.

Don John. [*Aside*] What magical illusion's this? 'Tis she.
    [*To Catelina*] Confusion seize your charitable blindness;
    Are you a prison visitor for this,   85
    To cherish my dishonour for your merit?
Catelina. My Lord, I hope my charity works for your honour,
    Relieving him whose mercy spared your life.
Don John. But that I'm subject to the law, and know
    My blows are mortal, I would strike thee dead.   90
    Ignoble and degenerate from Spanish blood,
    Darest thou maintain this to be charity?
    Thy strumpet itch, and treason to my bed,
    Thou seek'st to act in cherishing this villain.
Catelina. Saints be my witnesses, you do me wrong.   95
Don John. Thou robb'st my honour.
Pike. You wound her honour and you rob yourself,
    And me, and all good Christians by this outrage.
Don John. Do you prate, sir?
Pike. Sir, I may speak; my tongue's unshackled yet,   100
    And were my hands and feet so, on free ground,
    I would maintain the honour of this lady
    Against an host of such ignoble husbands.
Don John. You are condemned already by the law,
    I make no doubt, and therefore speak your pleasure,   105
    And here come those for whom my rage is silent.

Enter FERNANDO, TENIENTE, Guard.

Fernando. Deliver up your prisoner to the Teniente.
    I need not, sir, instruct you in your place,
    To bear him with a guard, as is appointed,
    Unto the public trial held at Jerez.   110
Teniente. It shall be done.

---

92. darest] *this ed.; perhaps* dar'st *Q;* darst *Malone.*

---

106. *for*] because of.

84 DICK OF DEVONSHIRE [ACT 3

Fernando. [*To the Jailer*] How long hath he been your
                                        prisoner?
Jailer. Eighteen days.
Fernando. You and the surgeons out of the King's pay
    I'll see discharged. You have, according to the order,   115
    Conveyed already Bustamente thither
    To yield account for yielding up the castle?
Teniente. 'Tis done, my Lord.
Fernando. Don John, you likewise, in his Majesty's name,
    Stand charged to make your personal appearance   120
    To give in evidence against this prisoner.
Don John. I shall be ready there, my Lord.
Pike. To Jerez? They say the best sack's there. I mean to take
    one draught of dying comfort.
Catelina. I hope you'll not deny my company to wait on you   125
    to Jerez?
Don John. No. You shall go to see your friend there totter.
Pike. I have a suit, my Lord, to see an Englishman,
    A merchant, prisoner here, before I go.
Fernando. Call him. That done, you know your charge.   130
                            Exit JAILER.
Teniente. And shall perform it.
                Exeunt FERNANDO, DON JOHN, CATELINA.

                Enter JAILER *and* WOODROW.

Pike. Oh, Mr. Woodrow, I must now take leave
    Of prison fellowship with you. Your fortunes
    May call you into England, after payment
    Of some few money debts, but I am called   135
    Unto a further trial. My debt is life,
    Which if they take not by extortion,
    I mean by tortures, I shall gladly pay it.
Woodrow. I have heard, and thought you, by what I had
                                        heard,
    Free from fear's passion; still continue so,   140
    Depending on Heaven's mercy.

---

115. *discharged*] paid.
127. *totter*] swing from the gallows; be hanged (*OED* 1b).
140. *Free from fear's passion*] fearless.

SC 3]   DICK OF DEVONSHIRE   85

Pike. You do instruct me well; but, worthy countryman,
       Once more let me give you this to remember,
       And 'tis my last request: that when your better stars
       Shall guide you into England, you'll be pleased   145
       To take my country, Devonshire, in your way,
       Where you may find in Tavistock (whom I left)
       My wife and children wretched in my misfortunes.
       Commend me to them. Tell them, and my friends,
       That if I be, as I suspect I shall be,   150
       At Jerez put to death, I died a Christian soldier;
       No way, I hope, offending my just King,
       Nor my religion, but the Spanish laws.
                                                 Exeunt.

                            SCENE 3

            Enter DON PEDRO, *reading a letter, and* MANUELL.

Manuell. Dear sir, let me have power to recall
       Your graver thoughts, out of this violent storm
       Of passion, that thus overwhelms your mind.
       Remember what you are, and with what strength,
       What more than manly strength, you have outworn   5
       Dangers of battle, when your warlike looks
       Have outfaced horror.
Don Pedro.   Oh, my son, my son,
       Horror itself upon the wings of death
       Stretched to the uttermost expansion,
       Over the wounded body of an army,   10
       Could never carry an aspect like this,
       This murdering spectacle; this field of paper,
       Stuck all with Basilisks' eyes. Read but this word,
       The ravisht Eleonora. Does't not seem
       Like a full cloud of blood ready to burst   15
       And fall upon our heads?

---

152. *No way*] in no way.

11. *aspect*] appearance.
13. *Basilisks'*] A fabulous reptile alleged to be hatched by a serpent from
a cock's egg; ancient authors stated that its hissing drove away all other
serpents, and that its breath, and even its look, were fatal.

86 DICK OF DEVONSHIRE [ACT 3

Manuell. Indeed, you take too deep a sense of it.
Don Pedro. What? When I see this meteor hanging o'er it?
　　This prodigy in figure of a man
　　Clad all in flames, with an inscription　　　　　　　20
　　Blazing on's head: Henrico the Ravisher?
Manuell. Good sir, avoid this passion.
Don Pedro. In battles I have lost, and seen the falls,
　　Of many a right good soldier; but they fell
　　Like blessed grain that shot up into honour.　　　25
　　But in this lewd exploit I lose a son
　　And thou a brother, my Emanuell,
　　And our whole house the glory of her name.
　　Her beauteous name, that never was disdained,
　　Is, by this beastly fact, made odious.　　　　　　30
Manuell. I pray sir be yourself, and let your judgement
　　Entertain reason; from whom came this letter?
Don Pedro. From the sad plaintiff, Eleonora.
Manuell. 　　　　　　　　　　Good,
　　And by the common post; you, every week
　　Receiving letters from your noble friends,　　　　35
　　Yet none of their papers can tell any such tidings.
Don Pedro. All this may be too, sir.
Manuell. Why is her father silent? Has she no kindred,
　　No friend, no gentleman of note, no servant
　　Whom she may trust to bring by word of mouth　40
　　Her dismal story?
Don Pedro. 　　　　　　No, perhaps she would not
　　Text up his name in proclamations.
Manuell. Some villain hath filled up a cup of poison
　　T'infect the whole house of the Gusman family,
　　And you are greediest first to take it down.　　　45
Don Pedro. That villain is thy brother.
Manuell. 　　　　　　　　　Were you a stranger,
　　Armed in the middle of a great battalia

18–21. *When I ... on's head*] See Eleonora's reference to a 'prodigious comet' in 2.2.195.

41–2. *she would ... proclamations*] she would not write his name down in a public notice.

45. *take it down*] drink it.

47. *battalia*] order of battle, battle array; disposition or arrangement of troops for action (*OED* 1).

SC 3]   DICK OF DEVONSHIRE   87

And thus should dare to tax him, I would wave
My weapon o'er my head to waft you forth
To single combat. If you would not come,   50
Had I as many lives as I have hairs,
I'd shoot 'em all away to force my passage
Through such an host until I met the traitor
To my dear brother. Pray, do not think so, sir.
Don Pedro. Not? When it shall be said one of our name   55
(Oh Heaven, could I but say he were not my son)
Was so dishonourable, so sacrilegious, to defile a
                                                temple
Of such a beauty and goodness as she was?
Manuell. As beauteous is my brother in his soul
As she can be.
Don Pedro.   Why dost thou take his part so?   60
Manuell. Because no drop of honour falls from him
But I bleed with it. Why do I take his part?
My sight is not so precious as my brother.
If there be any goodness in one man,
He's lord of that; his virtues are full seas,   65
Which cast up to the shores of the base world
All bodies thrown into them. He's no drunkard.
I think he ne'er swore oath. To him, a woman
Was worse than any scorpion, till he cast
His eye on Eleonora; and therefore, sir,   70
I hope it is not so.
Don Pedro.   Was not she so?
Manuell. I do not say, sir, that she was not so,
Yet women are strange creatures. But my hope
Is that my brother was not so ignoble.
Good sir, be not too credulous on a letter.   75
Who knows but it was forged, sent by some foe,
As the most virtuous ever have the most.

---

48. *tax*] levy; i.e. enlist Henrico for battle.
him] i.e. Henrico.
  51. *Had I as many lives as I have hairs*] See *Macbeth* (1606), 5.7.90: 'Had
I as many sons as I have hairs, / I would not wish them to a fairer death.'
  63. *My sight ... brother*] My brother is more precious to me than my sight
is.
  71. *Was not she so?*] Was she not dishonoured?
  77. *the most*] the most enemies.

88　　　　　　　　DICK OF DEVONSHIRE　　　　　　　　[ACT 3

I know my brother loved her honour so
As wealth of kingdoms could not him entice
To violate it, or his faith to her.　　　　　　　　　　　80
Perhaps it is some quaint device of theirs
To haste your journey homeward out of France
To terminate their long-desired marriage.
Don Pedro. The language of her letter speaks no such
　　　　　　　　　　　　　　　　　　　　　comfort.
But I will hasten home; and for you are　　　　　85
So confident, as not to think his honour
Any way touched, your good hopes be your guide,
Auspiciously to find it to your wish.
Therefore, my counsel is you post before
And, if you find that such a wrong be done,　　　90
Let such provision instantly be
Betwixt you made to hide it from the world
By giving her due nuptial satisfaction,
That I may hear no voice of't at my coming.
Oh, to preserve the reputation　　　　　　　　95
Of noble ancestry that ne'er bore stain,
Who would not pass through fire, or dive the main?
　　　　　　　　　　　　　　　　　　　Exeunt.

SCENE 4

Enter FERNANDO *and* ELEONORA.

Fernando. Cease, Eleonora. Cease these needless plaints,
Less useful than thy help of hands was at
The deed of darkness; oh, the blackest deed
That ever overclouded my felicity.

---

80. her:] *Malone; perhaps* her. *Q.*

90–4. *if you ... coming*] If you should find that Henrico has raped
Eleonora, arrange for them to be married so that the matter is resolved by
the time I get home.

97. *dive the main*] possible reference to hazard, a game of risk in which
the chances are complicated by a number of arbitrary rules, and in which a
player had to 'throw a main' to win the stake.

1. *plaints*] complaints.

3. *deed of darkness*] i.e. the rape of Eleonora.

4.] Bullen offers 'That e'er o'erclouded', to preserve the iambic
pentameter.

sc 4]   DICK OF DEVONSHIRE   89

To speak or weep thy sorrow but allays   5
And quenches anger, which we must now cherish
To further just revenge. How I could wish
But to call back the strength of twenty years.
Eleonora. That I might be in that unborn again sir.
Fernando. No, Eleonora, that I were so enabled   10
With my own hands to work out thy revenge
Upon that wretch, that villain, oh that ravisher.
But, though my hands are palsied with rage,
The law yet wears a sword in our defence.

Enter HENRICO.

Eleonora. Away, my Lord and father; see the monster   15
Approaching towards you. Who knows but now
He purposeth an assassinate on your life
As he did lately on my virgin honour?
Fernando. Fury, keep off me.
Henrico. What life? What honour mean you? Eleonora,   20
What is the matter? Who hath lost anything?
Eleonora. Thou impudent, as impious, I have lost.
Henrico. Do you call me names?
Eleonora.   The solace of my life,
for which—
Henrico.   A fine new name for a maidenhead.
Eleonora. May all the curses of all injured women   25
Fall on thy head.
Henrico. Would not the curses of all good ones serve?
So many might perhaps be born. But pray,
Tell me what moves you thus? Why stand you so
Aloof, my Lord? I do not love to be   30
Used like a stranger; welcome's all I look for.
Fernando. What boldness beyond madness gives him
                            language?
Nothing but Hellbred stuff. Canst see my daughter
And not be struck with horror of thy shame
To th' very heart? Is't not enough, thou traitor,   35
To my poor girl's dishonour to abuse her,

---

35. th'[e] very] *Malone;* th'very *Q.*

9. *in that*] in that twenty-year regression.
25. *injured*] dishonoured.

90   DICK OF DEVONSHIRE   [ACT 3

But thou canst yet put on a devil's visor
To face thy fact, and glory in her woe?
Henrico. I would I were acquainted with your Honour's
    meaning all this while.   40
Fernando. The foreign enemy, which came to the city
    And twice danced on the sea before it, waving
    Flags of defiance and of fury to it,
    Were, nor before, nor now this second time,
    So cruel as thou; for when they first were here,   45
    Now well nigh forty years since, and marched through
    The very heart of this place, trampled on
    The bosoms of our stoutest soldiers,
    The women yet were safe. Ladies were free,
    And that by the especial command   50
    Of the then noble general; and now being safe
    From common danger of our enemies,
    Thou lion-like hast broke in on a lamb
    And preyed upon her.
Henrico.   How have I preyed?
Fernando. Dost thou delight to hear it named, villain?   55
    Th'hast ravisht her.
Henrico. I am enough abused, and now 'tis time
    To speak a little for myself, my Lord.
    By all the vows, the oaths and imprecations
    That ere were made, studied, or practisèd,   60
    As I have a soul, as she and you have souls,
    I do not know, nor can, nor will confess
    Any such thing; for all your circumventions,
    I'll answer all by law.
Eleonora. Oh my Lord, hear me. By all that's good—   65
Fernando. Peace, Eleonora, I have thought the course
    If you dare justify the accusation.
    You shall to Jerez, and then before the judges

41–2. *The foreign ... before it*] The English fleet that has invaded Spain
twice (i.e. in 1596 and 1625).
   43. *Flags of defiance*] See 1.3.46–7.
   59. *imprecations*] invocations of evil; curses.
   63. *circumventions*] entrapments.
   66. *course*] course of action.

SC 4]   DICK OF DEVONSHIRE   91

Plead your own cause.
Henrico.   And there I'll answer it.
Fernando. There, if you prove the rape, he shall be forced   70
    Either to satisfy you by marriage
    Or else to lose his perjured head.
Henrico.   I am content.
    And instantly I will away to Jerez,
    There to appeal to the High Court of Justice.
    'Tis time, I think, such slanderous accusations   75
    Assailing me, but there I shall be righted.
Fernando. You shall not need to doubt it. Come, Eleonora.
                                        Exeunt

Henrico. What will become of me in this I know not;
    I have a shrewd guess though of the worst.
    Would one have thought the foolish ape would put   80
    The finger in the eye, and tell it Daddy!
    'Tis a rare gift, 'mong many maids of these days;
    If she speed well, she'll bring it to a custom.
    Make her example followed to the spoil
    Of much good sport. But I mean to look to't.   85

                    Enter BUZZANO.

[*To Buzzano*] Now, sir, your news?
Buzzano. The most delicious, rare, absolute, news that e'er
    came out of France, sir.
Henrico. What's done there? Have they forsaken the devil and
    all his fashions? Banished their tailors and tirewomen?   90
Buzzano. You had a father and a brother there, and can you
    first think upon the devil and his limetwigs?

---

77. SD *Exeunt*] *Bullen (subst.)*; *Exit Q*; *Exit Malone*.

80–1. *Would one ... Daddy!*] If only I had thought that Eleonora would
run crying to her daddy with fake tears (i.e. tears brought about by poking
her finger in her eye).
    80. *foolish ape*] i.e. Eleonora.
    83–5. *If she ... sport*] If she succeeds, crying rape will become a custom,
and if other women follow her example, men will be denied a lot of
entertainment.
    90. *tirewomen*] both a lady's maid and a woman employed in the making
or sale of women's clothing; the latter would seem to be the most probable
definition, given its inclusion with 'tailors'.
    92. *limetwigs*] a twig smeared with birdlime for catching birds (*OED* 1b).

92   DICK OF DEVONSHIRE   [ACT 3

Henrico. Had, Buzzano? Had a father and a brother there?
　　Have I not so still, Buzzano?
Buzzano. No sir, your elder brother is—　　　　　　　95
Henrico. What? Speak Buzzano; I imagine dead.
Buzzano. Nay, you shall give me something by your leave. You
　　shall pay the post; good news for nothing?
Henrico. Here, here Buzzano. Speak quickly; crown me with
　　the felicity of a younger brother. Is he dead, man?　　100
Buzzano. No, he's come home very well sir. Do you think I
　　go on dead men's errands?
Henrico. Pox on the buzzard. How he startled my blood!
Buzzano. But he is very weary, and very pensive, sir; talks not
　　at all, but calls for his bed. Pray God your father be not　105
　　dead! And desires when you come in to have you his
　　bedfellow, for he hath private speech with you.
Henrico. Well sir, you that are so apt to take money for news,
　　beware how you reflect one word, syllable, or thought
　　concerning Eleonora. You know what I mean?　　　　110
Buzzano. Yes, and mean what you know, sir.
Henrico. What's that?
Buzzano. I'll keep your counsel.
Henrico. My life goes for it else.

　　　　　　　　　　　　　　　　　　　Exeunt.

Act 4

SCENE I

Enter HENRICO *(as newly risen).*

Henrico. [*Calling*] Buzzano? Slave? Buzzano?

Enter BUZZANO *with cloak and rapier.*

Buzzano. Signior, what a buzzing you make! As if you were a
fly at Bartholomewtide at a butcher's stall. Do you think
I am deaf?

Henrico. No, but blind. Do'st sleep as thou goest?   5

Buzzano. No, but I go as I sleep, and that's scurvily.

Henrico. Call my brother, Manuell.

Buzzano. [*Calling*] Brother Manuell.

Henrico. How? Pray (goodman rascal), how long have he and
you been brothers?   10

Buzzano. I know not. Maybe ever since we were born, for
your father used to come home to my mother; and why
may not I be a chip of the same block out of which you
two were cut? Mothers are sure of their children, but no
man is able to swear who was his father.   15

Henrico. You are very lusty.

Buzzano. I ate eringoes and potched eggs last night.

Henrico. Go and call him.

Buzzano. What?

Henrico. You hound, is he up?   20

Buzzano. No, he's in bed, and yet he may be up too; I'll go
see.

Henrico. Stay, and speak low.

---

2. *buzzing*] Buzzano plays upon Henrico's repeated calling of his name.

3. *Bartholomewtide*] a festival celebrated on 24 August.

17. *eringoes*] a sweetmeat regarded as an aphrodisiac (*OED* 1). See also
The Merry Wives of Windsor (5.5.16).

potched] poached.

93

94   DICK OF DEVONSHIRE   [ACT 4

BUZZANO *falls down.*

How now?

Buzzano. I can speak no lower unless I creep into the cellar.   25

Henrico. I'm glad you are so merry, sir.

Buzzano. So am I. My heart is a fiddle; the strings are rosened
     with joy that my other young master is come home, and
     my tongue is the stick that makes the fiddle squeak.

Henrico. Come hither; leave your fooling and tell me truly,   30
     didst sleep tonight or no?

Buzzano. Sleep? Not that I remember. I'll swear, and my eyes
     should come out as two witnesses, that I ne'er slept
     worse, for what with your Spanish flies (the pocky sting-
     ing mosquitoes) and what with your skip jack fleas, the   35
     nap of my sleep was worn off.

Henrico. Didst hear nothing?

Buzzano. Not in my sleep.

Henrico. Collect thy senses. When thou wert awake, didst thou
     hear nothing?   40

Buzzano. Nothing.

Henrico. 'Twixt twelve and one?

Buzzano. Twelve and one? Then was I in my dead sleep,
     cursing the fleas.

Henrico. Or about one and two?   45

Buzzano. That's three. Now the beetle of my head beats it
     into my memory that as you and your brother, Manuell,
     lay in the high bed, and I trundling underneath, I heard
     one of you talk most stigmatically in his sleep; most
     horriferously.   50

Henrico. Right. Now thou com'st to me, so did I.

Buzzano. And then once or twice the sleepy voice cried out,
     'Oh, it was I that murdered him; this hand killed him.'

Henrico. Art sure thou heardst this?

Buzzano. Am I sure these are my ears?   55

Henrico. And darest thou swear thou heardst it?

Buzzano. Lay down twenty oaths and see if I'll not take them.

---

   29. *stick*] bow.

   48. *trundling*] occupying a trundle- or truckle-bed, a low bed on castors,
stored underneath a higher bed. See Middleton's *A Game at Chess* (1625),
2.1.194: 'He's laid 'em all in truckle-beds methinks.'

   49. *stigmatically*] villainously.

SC I]   DICK OF DEVONSHIRE   95

Henrico. And whose voice was it did appear to thee?

Buzzano. Whose was it? Well said, young master; make an ass
    of your father's man.   60

Henrico. Come, come, be serious; whose voice?

Buzzano. Whose voice? Why then, if your windpipe were slit
    now and opened, there should the voice be found. I durst,
    at midnight, be sworn that the ghost of your voice
    appeared before me.   65

Henrico. No, me it frighted too; up stood my hair, stiff and
    on end.

Buzzano. As a cat's does at sight of a dog.

Henrico. A cold sweat (pearled in drops) all o'er my body; for
    'twas my brother's voice, and were I called before a thou-   70
    sand judges, I must swear it could be no man's else.

Buzzano. Why then, I must swear so too.

Henrico. 'Oh, it was I that murdered him, this hand killed
    him.'

Manuell. [*within*] Buzzano?   75

Henrico. He's up.

Manuell. Buzzano?

Buzzano. I come.

Henrico. Help to make him ready, but not a word on thy life.

Buzzano. Mum.   *Exit* BUZZANO.   80

Henrico. So let it work; thus far my wheels go true,
    Because a captain leading up his men
    In the proud van has honour above them,
    And they his vassails, must my elder brother
    Leave me a slave to the world! And why, forsooth?   85
    Because he got the start in my mother's belly;
    To be before me there. All younger brothers
    Must sit beneath the salt and take what dishes

---

80. *Mum*] agreement to keep 'mum' i.e silent (the full colloquialism being
'mum's the counsel', a precursor to the later 'mum's the word').

81. *true*] straight.

83. *van*] See 2.4.44.

84. *vassails*] in the feudal system, one holding lands from a superior on
conditions of homage and allegiance; a feudatory; a tenant in fee.

88. *beneath the salt*] to sit at the lower part of the table, i.e. among the less
honoured guests. The reference is to the formerly prevailing custom of
placing a large salt-cellar in the middle of a dining table. See also Dekker
and Middleton's *Honest Whore* (1604) (*OED* 7b).

96 DICK OF DEVONSHIRE [ACT 4

The elder shoves down to them. I do not like
This kind of service; could I, by this trick 90
Of a voice counterfeited, and confessing
The murder of my father, truss up this yonker
And so make my self heir and a younger brother
Of him, 'twere a good day's work. were't not fine angling?
Hold line and hook, I'll puzzle him. 95

Enter MANUELL *and* BUZZANO.

Manuell. Morrow, brother.
Henrico. Oh, good morrow. You have slept soundly.
Manuell. Travellers that are weary have sleep led in a string.
Buzzano. [*Aside*] So do those that are hanged. [*To Manuell*]
All that travel and are weary do not sleep. 100
Manuell. Why, Mr Buzzano, why?
Buzzano. Midwives travel at night and are weary with eating
groaning pie, and yet sleep not. Shall I hook you?
Manuell. Hook me? What meanst?
Buzzano. These tailors are the wittiest knaves that live by 105
bread.
Henrico. And why witty? Out of your wisdom.
Buzzano. In old time, gentlemen would call to their men, and
cry, 'Come truss me'. Now the word is, 'come hook me',
for every body now looks so narrowly to tailor's bills 110
(some, for very anger, never paying them) that the needle
lance knights in revenge of those prying eyes, put so many
hooks and eyes to every hose and doublet.
Manuell. Well, sir, I'll not be hooked then now.
Buzzano. 'Tis well if you be not. *Exit.* 115

---

92. *yonker*] a young nobleman or gentleman.
103–13. *Shall I ... doublet*] The tailors, the 'needle lance knights', are
adding superfluous fastenings to clothing to increase their bills. As garments
assumed increasing transience with changing fashions throughout the seventeenth century, so the figure of the tailor, the creator of such garments,
was portrayed as morally suspect, with greater concern for making money
than for the practicality of the clothing. See introduction, p. 20.
103. *hook you*] fasten your hose and doublet. Here, Buzzano also alludes
to Henrico's plan to set Manuell up for Don Pedro's murder. The tailor
manipulating his clients is analogous with Henrico's manipulation of his
father's absence for his own gain.

SC I]   DICK OF DEVONSHIRE   97

Henrico. France is an excellent country?
Manuell.   Oh, a brave one.
Henrico. Your monsieurs gallant sparks?
Manuell.   Sparks? Oh sir, all fire.
 The soul of compliment, courtship and fine language,
 Witty and active lovers of fair ladies,
 Short nags, and English mastifs. Proud, fantastic,   120
 Yet such a pride, and such fantasticness,
 It so becomes them, other nations
 (Especially the English) hold themselves
 No perfect gentlemen till Frenchified.
Henrico. Tush, England breeds more apes than Barbary.   125
 How chance my father came not home with you?
Manuell. He was too hard tied by the leg with business.
Henrico. What business?
Manuell.   'Tis but stepping into France,
 And he perhaps will tell you.
Henrico.   Perhaps? 'Tis well.
 What part of France did you leave him in?   130
Manuell. What part? Why I left him at Nancy in Lorraine; no,
 no, I lie. Now I remember me; 'twas at Chaalons in
 Burgundy.
Henrico. Hoyda, a most loving child, that knows not where he
 left his father, and yet   135
 Comes but now from him. Had you left in France
 Your whore behind you, in your table books
 You would have set down the street's very name;
 Yes, and the bawdy sign, too.
Manuell.   Hum, you say well, sir.
 Now you are up to th'ears in bawdery   140
 Pray, tell me one thing brother. (I am sorry
 To put forth such a question) but speak truly;

---

 125. *England breeds more apes than Barbary*] The English are too primitive
to ever be as sophisticated, or advanced, as the French.
 Barbary] Pirates from the North African Barbary Coast frequently seized
Spanish ships during the seventeenth century, and carried out some land
raids as well.
 127. *hard tied by the leg*] tied up with (colloquial).
 134. *Hoyda*] exclamation of surprise or wonder.
 137. *table books*] notebooks.

98 DICK OF DEVONSHIRE [ACT 4

Have you not, in my father's absence, done
A piece of work, (not your best masterpiece)
But such an one as on the house of Gusman 145
Will pluck a vengeance, and on the good old man
(Our noble father) heap such hills of sorrow
To beat him into his grave?

Henrico. What's this, your foolery?

Manuell. Pray Heaven it prove so. Have not you defaced that 150
sweet and matchless goodness, Eleonora? Fernando's
daughter?

Henrico. How defaced her?

Manuell. Hark sir, played Tarquin's part and ravisht her?

Henrico. 'Tis a lie. 155

Manuell. I hope so too.

Henrico. What villain speaks it?

Manuell. One with so wide a throat that uttering it 'twas heard
in France; a letter, sir, informed my father so.

Henrico. Letter? From whom?

Manuell.   A woman.

Henrico.   She's a whore. 160

Manuell. 'Twas Eleonora.

Henrico. She's then a villanous strumpet so to write,
And you an ass, a coxcomb, to believe it.

Manuell. Nettled? Then let me tell you that I fear
I shall forever blush when in my hearing 165
Any names Henrico Gusman for my brother.
In right of virtue and a woman's honour
(This dear wronged lady's) I dare call thee villain.

Henrico. Villain?

They fight.

Enter FERDINAND *and* Attendants.

Ferdinand. Part them, part them.

Henrico.   Let me see his heart 170
Panting upon my weapon's point, then part us;

---

154. *Tarquin's part*] Tarquin was the seventh, and traditionally last, King
of Rome. His son, Sextus, was alleged to have raped a noblewoman, resulting
in the expulsion of the Tarquin family from Rome, and the abolition of the
monarchy at Rome.

SC I]   DICK OF DEVONSHIRE   99

Else pray forbear the room.
Ferdinand.   Fie, fie, two brothers,
Two eaglets of one noble aery,
Peck out each other's eyes? Welcome from France.
How does your honoured father?
Manuell.   Well, my Lord;   175
I left him late in Paris.
Henrico.   So, so, in Paris;
Hath he three bodies? Lorraine? Burgundy? And Paris?
My Lord, his Highness, puts into your hand
A sword of justice. Draw it forth, I charge you
By th'oath made to your king, to smite this traitor,   180
The murderer of my father.
Manuell.   I?
Henrico.   Yes, thou.
Thou, slave, hast been his executioner.
Manuell. Where? When?
Henrico.   There, then, in France.
Manuell.   Oh, Heavenly powers!
Henrico. Oh, intolerable villain, parasite, monster of
                              mankind, Spaniard's shame.
Ferdinand. Pray, hear me, are you in earnest?   185
Henrico. Earnest.
Ferdinand. Be advised.
Henrico. Lay hold on him, the murderer of my father;
I have armed proofs against him.
Manuell.   An armed devil,
And that's thy self; produce thy proofs.
Henrico.   I will, sir,   190
But I will do't by law.
Ferdinando.   You are up already
Too deep, I fear, in law.
Henrico.   If you can, set then
Your foot upon my head and drown me; your worst.
Let me have justice here.
Ferdinand.   Well, sir, you shall.

---

172. *forbear*] leave.
177. *Hath he ... Paris*] This refers back to lines 131–3, when Manuell gives
conflicting accounts of his father's whereabouts.
193. *your worst*] do your worst.

100   DICK OF DEVONSHIRE   [ACT 4

Manuell, I can no less than lay upon you   195
The hand of my authority; in my carriage
You shall with me to Jerez, three leagues off,
Where the Lords sit tomorrow. There you must answer
This most unbrotherly accusation.
Manuell. And prove him a false caitiff.   200
Ferdinand. I will be both your guard, sir, and your bail
And make no doubt to free you from this viper.
Henrico. Viper?
Ferdinand.   Y'are bound to appear at Jerez, sir,
And you were best not fail.
I have a certain daughter there shall meet you. Come.   205
       [*Exeunt* FERDINAND, MANUELL, *and* Attendants]
Henrico. Thither I dare you both, all three. Buzzano?
Buzzano. Sir?
Henrico. Saddle my jennet; I'll to Jerez presently.
Buzzano. And I?
Henrico. And you; but I must school you, sirrah.   210
                       Exeunt.

SCENE 2

Enter PIKE, *shackled, and his* JAILER.

Jailer. Buon coragio, man; how is't?
Pike. Not very well, and yet well enough, considering how the
     cheating dice of the world run.
Jailer. I dare not, though I have a care of you, ease you of one
     iron unless I desire such gyves myself.   5
Pike. 'Las, if they were all knockt off, I'm loaden with gyves,
     shackles and fetters enough for the arrantest thief that
     ever lay in my own country in Newgate.

205.1. SD *Exeunt ...* ATTENDANTS] *this ed.; Exit. cu Man & suis Q.*

---

200. *caitiff*] wretch.

1. *Buon coragio*] an Italian greeting, literally 'good courage'.
2–3. *and yet ... world run*] and yet it could be worse in the circumstances.
5. *gyves*] shackles for the leg.
8. *Newgate*] Newgate Prison in London. Newgate was also used as a
generic term to refer to any English prison.

| SC 2] | DICK OF DEVONSHIRE | 101 |

Jailer. Shackles, gyves, and fetters enough? I see none but
these at your heels, which come on without a shoeing   10
horn.

Pike. Yes, at my heart I wear them; a wife and children (my
poor lambs, at home). There's a chain of sighs and sobs,
and sorrow, harder than any iron, and this chain is so long
it reaches from Jerez to Tavistock, in Devonshire.   15

Jailer. That's far enough in conscience.

Pike. Could I shake those chains off I would cut capers; poor
Dick Pike would dance, though death piped to him. Yes,
and spit in your hangman's face.

Jailer. Not too much of that neither. Some two days hence,   20
he will give you a choke pear will spoil your spitting.

Pike. Phew.

Jailer. For let me see; today is Sunday. Tomorrow the Lords
sit, and then I must have a care, a cruel care, to have your
legs handsome, and a new clean ruff band about your   25
neck, of old rusty iron. 'Twill purge your choler.

Pike. I, I, let it, let it. Collars, halters and hangmen are to me
bracelets and friendly companions.

Knocking within.

Jailer. So hasty; stay my leisure.

Enter two FRIARS.

Two friars come to prepare you.   *Exit.*   30

1 Friar. Hail, countryman, for we, though friars in Spain,
Were born in Ireland.

Pike.   Reverend sir, y'are welcome.
Too few such visitants, nay none at all,
Have I seen in this damnable limbo.

2 Friar. Brother, take heed; do not misuse that word of limbo.   35

1 Friar. Brother Pike, for so we hear men call you, we are
come in pure devotion and charity to your soul, being
thereto bound by holy orders of our mother church.

14–15. *chain ... Devonshire*] The play's repeated use of the analogy of
shackles with jewellery is set out in the introduction, p. 21.

17. *cut capers*] dance (*OED* a).

21. *choke pear*] figurative; something difficult or impossible to swallow.

102   DICK OF DEVONSHIRE   [ACT 4

Pike. What to do, pray, with me?
1 Friar.   To point with our fingers
    Out all such rocks, shelves, quicksands, gulfs and shallows   40
    Lying in the sea through which you are to pass
    In the most dangerous voyage you e'er made;
    Either by our care to set you safe on land,
    Or, if you fly from us, your Heavenly pilots,
    Sure to be wrackt for ever.
Pike.   What must I do?   45
2 Friar. Confess to one of us what rank and foul
    Impostumes have bred about your soul.
1 Friar. What leprosies have run o'er all your conscience.
2 Friar. What hot fevers now shake your peace of mind.
1 Friar. For we are come to cure your old corruptions.   50
2 Friar. We are come to be your true and free physicians.
1 Friar. Without the hope of gold to give you health.
2 Friar. To set you on your feet on the right way,
1 Friar. To Palestine, the new Jerusalem.
2 Friar. Say, will you unlock the closet of your heart   55
    To one of us? Choose which, and be absolved
    For all your black crimes on a free confession?
1 Friar. To him, or me, for you must die tomorrow.
Pike. Welcome; tomorrow shall I be in another country, where
    are no examiners, nor jailers, nor bolts, nor bars nor irons.   60
    I beseech you give me a little respite to retire into the
    next room and I will instantly return to give you satisfac-
    tion.   *Exit.*
Both. Go, brother.
1 Friar. A goodly man.   65
2 Friar. Well limbed, and strong of heart.
1 Friar. Now I well view his face, did not we two
    At our last being in Plymouth in disguise,
    When there the King of England rode about
    To see the soldiers in their musterings,   70

---

64. SH *Both*] *this ed.; Ambo Q; Ambo Malone.*

42. *the most dangerous voyage*] i.e. the journey from mortal life on earth
to eternal life in Heaven.
    70. *musterings*] assemblies of soldiers.

SC 2]   DICK OF DEVONSHIRE   103

And what their arms were, just before this fleet
Set out, did we not see him there?
2 Friar. Maybe we did. I know not, if he were there; 'tis now
out of my memory.

Enter PIKE.

1 Friar. Are you resolved?
Pike.   Yes.
2 Friar.   To confess?
Pike.   I ha'done 't already.   75
1 Friar. To whom?
Pike.   To one who is in better place,
And greater power, than you to cure my sick,
Infected part, though maladies as infinite
As the sea sands, the grassy spears on earth,
Or as the drops of rain and stars in the firmament,   80
Stuck on me, he can clear all, cleanse me thoroughly.
2 Friar. You will not then confess?
Pike. No, I confess I will not.
1 Friar. We are sorry for you. For country's sake this counsel
do I give you: 85
When y'are before the Lords, rule well your tongue.
Be wary how you answer, least they trip you;
For they know the whole number of your ships,
Burden, men and munition, as well as you in England.
Pike. I thank you both.   90
2 Friar. Prepare to die.   *Exeunt* FRIARS.
Pike. I will so. Prepare to die? An excellent bell, and it sounds
sweetly. He that prepares to die, rigs a goodly ship; he
that is well prepared is ready to launch forth; he that
prepares well, and dies well arrives at a happy haven.   95
Prepare to die? Preparation is the sauce, death the meat,
my soul and body the guests, and to this feast will I go
boldly as a man, humbly as a Christian, and bravely as

---

75. *Are you resolved?*] Have you decided?
84. *counsel*] advice.
87. *trip you*] catch you in a lie.
92. *An excellent bell*] We might use the colloquialism, 'it has a good ring
to it'.

104   DICK OF DEVONSHIRE   [ACT 4

an Englishman. Oh my children, my children; my poor
wife and children!   100

    Enter JAILER, *and three* SPANISH PICAROES *chained.*

Jailer. Here's a cheerful morning towards, my brave bloods.
1 Picaro. Yes, Jailer, if thou wert to be hanged in one of our
rooms.
Jailer. On, on; the Lords will sit presently.
2 Picaro. What's he?   105
Jailer. An Englishman.
3 Picaro. A dog.
1 Picaro. A devil.
2 Picaro. Let's beat out his brains with our irons.
Jailer. On, on; leave railing, cursing, and lying. Had you not   110
run from the castle, the hangman and you had been hail
fellow well met. On.
All. Crows peck thy eyes out, English dog, curr, toad,
Hellhound.   *Exeunt.*
Pike. Patience is a good armour; humility a strong headpiece.   115
Would I had you all three I know where.

    Enter BUSTAMENTE *shackled and* JAILER.

Bustamente. Whither dost lead me?
Jailer. To a room by your self. 'Tis my office to have a care of
my nurse-children.
Bustamente. I have worn better Spanish garters. Thus rewarded   120
for my service?
Jailer. See, Captain Bustamente, do you know this fellow?
Bustamente. No.
Jailer. The Englishman brought prisoner into the city, and
from thence hither.   125
Pike. Oh Captain, I saw you at the fort perform the part of a
man.

---

    105. *What's he?*] Who's he?
    110–12. *Had you ... met*] You (the picaro) would have been hanged
already, had you not run away.
    111–12. *hail fellow well met*] intimate friends.
    116. *all three*] all three picaroes.
    119. *nurse-children*] the prisoners being looked after by the jailer.

SC 3]   DICK OF DEVONSHIRE   105

Bustamente. And now thou seest me acting the part of a slave.
 Farewell, soldier. I did not hate thee at the fort, though
 there we met enemies, and if thou and I take our leaves   130
 at the gallows, prithee let's part friends.
Jailer. Come along you two.
Pike. Hand in hand, if the Captain please. Noble Bustamente,
 at the winning of the fort, we had a brave breakfast.
Bustamente. True, but I doubt we shall have worse cheer at   135
 dinner.
Jailer. When was ever any meat well dressed in the hangman's
 kitchen?

Exeunt.

SCENE 3

Enter FERNANDO *bareheaded, talking with the*
DUKE OF MACADA, DUKE GYRON, *the* DUKE OF
MEDINA, *the* MARQUESSE D'ALQUEVEZZAS,
two GENTLEMEN, *one with Pike's sword, which is laid
on a table;* JAILER, TENIENTE; CLERK *with papers.*

Macada. Where's the Teniente?
Clerk.   The Duke calls for you.
Teniente.   Here, my Lord.
Macada. 'Tis the King's pleasure that those fugitives
 Which basely left the fort should not be honoured
 With a judicial trial, but presently
 (Both those you have at home and these in Jerez)   5

128.] In MS Egerton 1994, a stage direction on the left-hand side of the
page here reads, 'A Table out, sword and papers' (4.2.128.1). This stage
direction prepares the field for the following scene, which begins with a
substantial centred stage direction, reading 'Ent: fernando bareheaded,
talking wth ye Duke of Macada. Duke Gyron, Medyna / Marquesse
d'Alquevezzes, 2 gent: one wth Pikes sword, whch is laid on a table, Teniente
/ Clarke with paper' (4.3), thereby strengthening the case for a playhouse
manuscript rather than one intended for private readership. See further
discussion in the introduction, pp. 13–17.

0.1 SD. FERNANDO bareheaded] Fernando is bareheaded in a display of
humility in the presence of the dukes.
1. *Where's the Teniente?*] This line implies that the Teniente's entrance is
slightly later than those of the other characters.

106 DICK OF DEVONSHIRE [ACT 4

To die by martial law.
Teniente. My Lord, I'll see it done.
Macada. Dispatch the rest here.
Jailer. Yes, my Lord. I'll bring them carefully together to end
the business.
Gyron. Bring Bustamente in. 10

Exit JAILER.

Macada. My Lords, here's Don Fernando, relates to me
Two stories full of wonder: one of his daughter,
Famed for her virtues, fair Eleonora,
Accusing Don Henrico, youngest son
To noble Pedro Gusman, of a rape; 15
Another of the same Henrico's, charging
His elder brother Manuell with the murder
Of Pedro Gusman, who went late to France.
Gyron. Are all the parties here?
Fernando. Yes.
Gyron. Bring them in.

Exit FERNANDO.

Enter JAILER, BUSTAMENTE, GUARD.

Macada. Bustamente. The King, our master, looking with
sharp eyes 20
Upon your traitorous yielding up the fort,
Puts off your trial here. You must abide
Longer imprisonment.
Bustamente. I have already quitted
Myself, my Lord, of that which you call treason,
Which had in any here (he doing the like) 25
Been a high point of honour.
Alquevezzes. These braves cannot save you.
Gyron. You must not be your own Judge.
Macada. You gave the English
More glory by your base ignoble rendering

---

18. *late*] recently.
23. *quitted*] acquitted.
24–5. *which ... like*] which, if it had been done by any of the nobility present.
26. *These braves*] this bravado.

DICK OF DEVONSHIRE

SC 3]   107

That fort up, than our nation got from them
In all our undertakings.
Bustamente.   Hear me, my Lords.   30
Macada. Sir, sir, w'have other anvils. Bustamente,
    Prepare yourself for death.
Bustamente.   For all my service!
All. Take him away.
Bustamente.   You are lions and I the prey.

         Exit BUSTAMENTE *with the* JAILER.

Macada. Which are Don Pedro's sons?

         Enter FERNANDO, HENRICO, MANUELL.

Fernando.   These two.
Macada. Which youngest?
Henrico.   I, my Lord.   35

              Enter JAILER.

Macada. You charge this gentleman, your elder brother,
    with murder of your father.
Henrico.   Which I can prove.
Macada. And hither flies a ravisht lady's voice
    To charge you with a rape; the wronged daughter
    Of this most noble gentleman.
Henrico.   Let them prove that.   40
Macada. These accusations and the proofs shall meet
    Here face to face, in th' afternoon. Meantime,
    Pray, Don Fernando, let it be your care to see
    These gentlemen attended on by a strong guard.
Fernando. The wrongs done to myself waken me, my lord,
                                        to that.   45
Manuell. I would your Graces would hear me speak a little.
All. You shall have time.
Medina.   Take them away,
    And at their trial have the lady here.

    Exeunt FERNANDO, HENRICO, MANUELL, *and* JAILER.

---

32. *For all my service!*] After everything I have done!
45. *to that*] to the need to do that.
48. *the lady*] Eleonora.

108   DICK OF DEVONSHIRE   [ACT 4

Gyron. Where is the Englishman?
Clerk.   The Englishman?
Alquevezzes. What do you call him? Dick of Devonshire?   50
Medina. Because he is a soldier, let him have
    A soldier's honour. Bring him from his prison
    Full in the face of the whole town of Jerez,
    With drums and muskets.
Macada. How many soldiers are in the town?   55
Clerk. Five thousand.
Medina. Let two hundred march hither along with him as
                                        his guard.
    Where's the Teniente?
Teniente.   Here my Lord.
Medina. Pray see this done, and in good order.
Teniente.   I shall.   *Exit.*

                    Enter DON JOHN *below.*

Gyron. What makes Don John here? Oh, now I remember;   60
    You come against the Englishman.
Don John.   Yes, my Lord.

            Enter CATELINA *and a* GENTLEWOMAN *above.*

Macada. Give me the note there of the English advertisement.

                        They all confer.

Catelina. Here may we see and hear, poor Englishman,
    Sadness I cast on thee a noble pity;
    A pity mixed with sorrow, that my husband   65
    Has drawn him to this misery, to whom
    The soldier gave life, being at his mercy.

---

63. SH *Catelina*] *this ed.; Lad: Q. Amended as such from this point forward.*

---

    60. *What makes Don John here?*] What brings Don John here?
    62. *English advertisement*] written statement of instruction about Dick
Pike.
    63. SH] In MS Egerton 1994, the speech headings relating to Catelina
from hereon appear as 'Lady'.
    66–7. *to whom ... mercy*] Pike saved Don John's life, when Don John was
at Pike's mercy.

SC 3]   DICK OF DEVONSHIRE   109

Gentlewoman. 'Twas bravely done; no doubt he'll speed the
　　better for his mind.
Catelina. I visited him in prison and did, with much ado, win　　70
　　from Don John
　　This journey; for I vowed to see th'event
　　How they will deal with him.
Gentlewoman.　　　　　　　I hope most fairly.

　　　Enter two drums, TENIENTE, *diverse muskets,*
　　　　　　　FERNANDO *with*

　　　PIKE *(without band, an iron about his neck,*
　two chains manackling his wrists, a great chain at
　　　　his heels); JAILER, *3 or 4 halberts.*

　　　　　A bar set out.

Clerk. Silence.
Macada. You see how much our Spanish soldiers love you　　75
　　To give this brave attendance, though your nation
　　Fought us, and came to hunt us to our deaths.
Pike. My Lords, this, which in show, is brave attendance
　　And love to me, is the world's posture right;
　　Where one man's falling down sets up another.　　80
　　My sorrows are their triumphs so in King's court,
　　When officers are thrust out of their rooms
　　Others leap laughing in while they do mourn.
　　I am at your mercy.
Macada.　　　　　Sirrah Englishman,
　　Know you that weapon? Reach it him.　　85
Pike. Yes, it was once mine, and draws tears from me to think
　　how 'twas forced from me.
Macada. How many Spaniards killed you with that sword?

　　68–9. *no doubt ... mind]* no doubt the recollection of the mercy he showed
will help him to fare better at trial.
　　68. *speed]* fare.
　　69. *mind]* recollection.
　　76. *brave]* fine.
　　78. *in show]* on the surface.
　　88. *killed you]* did you kill.

110   DICK OF DEVONSHIRE   [ACT 4

Pike. Had I killed one, this bar had ne'er been guilty of my
pleading before such princely judges. There stands the   90
man.
Gyron. Don John, set he on you, or you on him?
Don John. He upon me first.
Pike. Let me then be torn into a thousand pieces.
Catelina. My husband speaks untruth.   95
Alquevezzes. Set he on you first? More coward you to suffer
an enemy be aforehand.
Pike. Indeed in England, my countrymen are good at bidding
stand, but I was not now upon a robbery, but a defence,
set round with a thousand dangers. He set upon me; I   100
had him at my feet, saved him, and for my labour was
after basely hurt by him.
Fernando. This was examined by me, my Lords,
And Don John, thus accused, was much ashamed
Of his unmanly dealing.
Gyron.   He may be now so.   105
Catelina. I blush for him myself.
Alquevezzes.   Disgrace to Spaniards.
Macada. Sirrah, you English, what was the ship you came in?
Pike. The Convertine.
Macada. What ordnance did she carry?
Pike. Forty pieces.   110
Gyron. No, sir, but thirty-eight; see here, my Lord.
Alquevezzes. Right, no more than thirty-eight.
Macada. Your fort at Plymouth strong?
Pike. Yes, very strong.
Macada. What ordnance in't?   115
Pike. Fifty pieces.
Gyron. Oh fie, do not belie your country; there's not so many.
Alquevezzes. How many soldiers keep you in that fort?
Pike. Two hundred.
Macada. Much about such a number. There is a little island 120
before Plymouth. What strength is that of?

96–7. *More coward ... aforehand*] More coward you to allow an enemy to
speak first.
98–9. *bidding stand*] bidding 'Stand and deliver', the infamous demand of
the highwayman robber.
103. *examined*] investigated.

SC 3]   DICK OF DEVONSHIRE   111

Pike. I do not know.
Gyron. We do then.
Alquevezzes. Is Plymouth a walled town?
Pike. Yes, it is walled.   125
Macada. And a good wall?
Pike. A very good strong wall.
Gyron. True; 'tis a good strong wall, and built so high
        One with a leap staff may leap over it.
Macada. Why did not your great navy, being in such bravery 130
        As it took Puntal, seize Cadiz?
Pike.   Our General
        Might easily have ta'en it, for he had
        Almost a thousand scaling ladders to set up,
        And, without maim to's army, he might lose
        A thousand men; but he was loath to rob   135
        An almshouse when he had a richer market
        To buy a conquest in.
Macada.   What was that market?
Pike. Genoa, or Lisbon. Wherefore should we venture
        Our lives to catch the wind? Or to get knocks
        And nothing else?   140

                    They consult.

Macada. A post with speed to Lisbon, and see't well manned.
Teniente. One shall be sent my Lord.   *Exit*

                    The soldiers laugh.

Alquevezzes. How now? Why is this laughter?
Fernando. One of the soldiers, being merry among themselves
        is somewhat bold with th'English, and says th'are
                                            dainty hens. 145

---

   124. *walled town*] Plymouth's town walls were first built in the 1530s, and
further strengthened in the 1590s when the new fort was being built.
   133. *scaling ladders*] ladders used in the assault of fortified places.
   134. *to's*] to his.
   lose] take.
   141. *A post ... manned*] i.e. a series of men stationed at suitable places
along the appointed post road, the duty of each being to ride forward speedily to the next stage, to bear the message of the possible approach of the
English to Lisbon.

112   DICK OF DEVONSHIRE   [ACT 4

All. Hens? Ha, ha, ha.
Macada.   Sirrah, view well these soldiers,
    And freely tell us, think you these will prove
    Such hens as are your English when the next year
    They land in your own country?
Pike.   I think they will not,
    My lord, prove hens, but somewhat near to hens.   150
Macada. How mean'st thou?
Pike.   Let my speech breed no offence;
    I think they would prove pullets.
Gyron.   Darest thou fight
    With any one of these, our Spanish pullets?
Pike. What heart have I to fight, when 'tis beaten flat
    To earth with sad afflictions? Can a prisoner   155
    Glory in playing the fencer? My life's at stake
    Already; can I put it in for more?
    Our army was some fourteen thousand men,
    Of which more than twelve thousand had spirits so high
    Mine never shall come near them. Would some of them   160
    Were here to feed your expectations.
    Yet, silly as I am, having fair pardon
    From all your graces and your greatnesses,
    I'll try, if I have strength in this chained arm,
    To break a rapier.
Macada.   Knock off all his gyves,   165
    And he that has a stomach for Spain's honour
    To combat with this Englishman, appear.
Pike. May he be never called an Englishman
    That dares not look a devil in the face.

One steps forth.

    Come he in face of man; come how he can.   170
Macada. Your name?
Tiago.   Tiago.
All.   Well done, Tiago.

---

152. *pullets*] young hens. Figuratively, here, young and inexperienced
soldiers.

154–7. *What heart ... more*] What is the point of fighting when I am
already likely to be sentenced to death?

156. *fencer*] gladiator.

SC 3] DICK OF DEVONSHIRE 113

Macada. Let drums beat all the time they fight.
Catelina. I pray for thee.
Gentlewoman.   And I.

> *They fight.* PIKE *disarms and trips him down.*

Pike. Only a Devonshire hug, sir;
  At your feet I lay my winnings.
Tiago.   Diablo.   175
> *Exit, biting his thumb.*

> *The* SOLDIERS *stamp.*

Gyron. Wilt venture on another?
Pike.   I beseech you
  To pardon me and task me to no more.
Alquevezzes. Come, come, one more. Look you; here's a
                      young cockerel
  Comes crowing into the pit.

> *Another steps in.*

All.   Prithee, fight with him.
Pike. I'm in the lion's grip, and to get from him   180
  There's but one way; that's death.
Macada. English, what say you? Will you fight or no?
Pike.   I'll fight.
Alquevezzes. Give 'em room; make way there.
Pike. I'll fight till every joint be cut in pieces
  To please such brave spectators. Yes, I'll fight   185
  While I can stand, be you but pleased, my Lords,
  The noble Dukes here, to allow me choice
  Of my own country weapon.
Alquevezzes.   What?
Pike. A quarterstaff, this, were the head off.
Macada. Off with the head, and room; how dost thou like
                      this, Spaniard? 190

175.1. Exit, biting his thumb] Bullen accounts the biting of the thumb
here as a mark of vexation, while noting that to bite one's thumb *at* a person
was considered an insult. See *Romeo and Juliet* (1597), I.1.34–40: 'No, sir, I
do not bite my thumb at you, sir, but I bite my thumb, sir.'
  182. *English*] Englishman.
  186–8. *be you ... weapon*] if you would let me choose my own weapon.
  189. *and room*] and give him room.

114   DICK OF DEVONSHIRE   [ACT 4

Pike. Well, he's welcome. Here's my old trusty friend. Are
                                    there no more?
    One? What, but one? Why I shall make no play,
    No sport, before my princely judges with one.
    More sacks to the mill. Come another; what, no more?
Macada. How many wouldst thou have?
Pike.   Any number under six.   195
All. Ha, ha, sure he's mad.
Macada.   Darest cope with three?
Pike. Where are they? Let 'em show their faces, so, welcome.
Macada. How dost thou like these chickens?
Pike. When I have drest them with sorrel sops, I'll tell you.

     Drums. They fight. One is killed, the other two disarmed.

Catelina. Now guard him, Heaven!
1 Soldier.   Hell take thy quarterstaff.   200
2 Soldier. Pox on thy quarters.

      A noise within of 'Diablo Englese'.

Macada.   The matter? Why this noise?
Jailer. The soldiers rail, stamp, and stare, and swear to cut
    His throat, for all the jailer's care of him.
Macada. Make proclamation, my Lord Fernando,
    That whosoever dares but touch his finger   205
    To hurt him, dies.
Fernando.   I will, sir.   *Exit.*
Catelina. This is done nobly.
Macada.   Here, give him this gold.
Teniente. The Duke of Macada gives you this gold.
Alquevezzes.   And this.
Teniente. The Duke of Medina this, Duke Gyron, this; and,
                            look you,
    the Marquess Alqueveza as much as all the rest.   210
Alquevezzes. Where's any of my men? Give him your cloak,
                              sirrah;
    Fetch him clean band and cuffs. I embrace thee, Pike,
    And hug thee in my arms. Scorn not to wear

---

    191. *my old trusty friend*] i.e. a quarterstaff.
    192. *but one?*] only one?
    203. *for all*] because of all.

SC 3]   DICK OF DEVONSHIRE   115

    A Spanish livery.
Pike.   Oh my Lord, I am proud of't.
Macada. He shall be with a convoy sent to the King.   215
Alquevezzes. Four of my gentlemen shall along with him.
    I'll bear thy charges, soldier, to Madrid;
    Five pieces of eight a day in travel and, lying still,
    Thou shalt have half that.
Pike.   On my knees, your vassal
    Thanks Heaven, you, and these princes.   220
Macada. Break up the court till after noon,
    Then the two Gusmans' trial.
All.   Come, Englishman.
Medina. How we honour valour thus our loves express,
    Thou hast a guard of Dukes and Marquesses.
                           Exeunt.

224. SD *Exeunt*] *this ed.; Exeunt all Q; Exeunt all Malone.*

219. *vassal*] See 4.1.84.

Act 5

SCENE I

Enter TENIENTE *and* HENRICO.

Teniente. The Lords are not yet risen; let us walk, and talk.
    Were not you better yield to marry her
    Than yield to suffer death? Know you the law?
Henrico. Law? Yes; the spider's cobweb, out of which great
    flies break, and in which the little are hanged, the tarriers,   5
    snaphance, limetwigs, weavers' shuttle and blanket in
    which fools and wrangling coxcombs are tossed. Do I
    know't now, or no?
Teniente. If of the rape she accuse you, 'tis in her choice
    To have you marry her, or to have you hanged.   10

---

6. snaphance] *Bullen (subst.);* snapsauce *Q.*

4–5. *Law ... hanged*] See Dekker's *Match Mee in London* (1611), 4.1.56–60: 'You oft call Parliaments, and there enact / Laws good and wholesome, such as who so break / Are hung by the purse or neck, but as the weak / And smaller flies i'th spider's web are tane / When great ones tear the web, and free remain.'

6. *snaphance*] armed robber or highwayman.

9–10. *If ... hanged*] Bullen cites two incidents from Anthony Copley's *Wits, Fits, and Fancies* (1614): 'One being condemned to be shot to death for a rape: the maid [*sic*] in favour of his life was content to beg him for her husband. Which being condiscended unto by the Judge, according to the lawe of Spaine in that behalfe: in steps me the hangman all in a chafe and said unto the Judge. Howe (I pray you, sir) can that be, seeing the stake is already in the ground, the rope, the arrowes, the Archers all in a readines, and heere I am come for him' (120); and, from the same collection, 'A fellow being to suffer, a maide came to the gallowes to beg him for her husband, according as the custome of Spaine dispenceth in that case. The people seeing this said unto the fellow: Now praise God that he hath thus mercifullie preserv'd thee, and see thou ever make much of this kinde woman that so friendly saves thy life. With that the Fellow viewing her and seeing a great skarre in her face, which did greatlie disfigure her, a long nose, thin lips and of a sowre complexion, hee said unto the Hangman: On (my good friend) doe thy duty: Ile none of her' (160).

SC 1] DICK OF DEVONSHIRE 117

Henrico. Hanged. Hanged, by any means. Marry her? Had I
   the King of Spain's seven kingdoms, Gallicia, Navarre,
   the two Castiles, Leon, Arragon, Valentia, Granada and
   Portugal to make up eight, I'd lose them all to be rid of
   such a piece of flesh.   15
Teniente. How, such a piece of flesh? Why, she has limbs
   Made out of wax.
Henrico.   Then have her to some fair,
   And show her for money.
Teniente.   Is she not sweet complexioned?
Henrico. As most ladies are that study painting.
Teniente. What meat will down your throat, when you scorn
                                         pheasant, 20
   partridge, woodcock and coney? Would I had such a
                                              dish!
Henrico. Woodcock and coney take to you, my Don Teniente,
   I'll none; and because you keep such a wondering, why
   my stomach goes against the wench (albeit I might find
   better talk, considering what ladder I stand upon), I'll tell 25
   you, Signior, what kind of wife I must have, or none.
Teniente. Pray, let me see her picture.
Henrico.   Draw then this curtain.
   Give me a wife that's sound of wind and limb,
   Whose teeth can tell her age, whose hand ne'er felt
   A touch lascivious, whose eyes are balls   30
   Not tossed by her to any but to me,
   Whose breath stinks not of sweetmeats, whose lips kiss
   Only themselves and mine, whose tongue ne'er lay
   At the sign of the bell. She must not be a scold,
   No, nor a fool to be in love with baubles,   35
   No, nor too wise, to think I ne'er sail true

17–18. *have her ... money*] Show her at a freak show, and charge people
money to see her. Freak shows were increasing in popularity in the royal
courts of Europe in the seventeenth century.

19. *As are ... painting*] Henrico implies that Eleonora's beauty is not
natural, but painted on, i.e. with cosmetics.

25. *ladder*] the ladder to the scaffold for execution, with a possible allusion
to Henrico's superior position on the social ladder.

27. *Let me see her picture*] Describe her to me.

35. *baubles*] trinkets, ornaments.

118   DICK OF DEVONSHIRE   [ACT 5

But when she steers the rudder. I'd not have
Her belly a drum, such as they weave points on,
Unless they be tagged with virtue. Nor would I have
Her white round breasts two sucking bottles to nurse   40
Any bastards at them.
Teniente.   I believe you would not.
Henrico. I would not have her tall, because I love not
To dance about a maypole, nor too low,
(Little clocks go seldom true). Nor, sir, too fat,
(Slug ships can keep no pace), no, nor too lean   45
To read anatomy lectures o'er her carcass.
Nor would I have my wife exceeding fair,
For then she's liquorish meat, and it would mad me
To see whoremasters teeth water at her.
Red haired by no means, though she would yield money   50
To sell her to some Jew for poison. No,
My wife shall be a globe terrestrial,
Moving upon no axeltree but mine;
Which globe when I turn round, what land soever
I touch my wife is with me, still I'm at home.   55
Teniente. But where will you find such a wife on earth?
Henrico. No, such a wife in the moon for me does tarry;
If none such shine here, I with none will marry.
Teniente. The Lords are come.
Henrico.   I care neither for lords nor ladies.

> *Enter the* Nobles *as before*; FERNANDO,
> MANUELL, CLERK, JAILER.

Macada. Where are these gentlemen? Set 'em both to a bar,   60
And opposite face to face. A confrontation

---

37. *But*] except.
44. *go seldom true*] rarely tell the correct time.
45. *Slug*] sluggish,
45–6. *too lean ... carcass*] so lean that you can see her skeleton.
48. *liquorish meat*] desirable by other men.
50–1. *Red haired ... poison*] In the seventeenth century, the fat of a red-haired man was thought to be an ingredient of poison. Compare Chapman's *Bussy D'Ambois* (1603): 'Worse than the poison of a red-hair'd man' (3.2.18).
52. *globe terrestrial*] globe with the countries printed on its surface.
53. *axeltree*] axis.
57. *such ... tarry*] I will not prolong the search by looking for such a wife in the moon.

SC I]   DICK OF DEVONSHIRE   119

May perhaps daunt th'offender, and draw from him
More than he'd utter. [*To Henrico*] You accuse your
                                                brother
As murderer of your father; where's your proof?
Henrico. First call my father's man in.
Clerk.   What's his name?   65
Henrico. Buzzano.
Clerk.   Call Buzzano in!

                    Enter BUZZANO.

Buzzano.   Here I am, here.
Clerk. Stand out. Whither go you?
Buzzano.   To stand out.
Clerk.   Stand there.
Macada. Now, what can he say?
Henrico.   First, my Lords, hear me.
    My brother and I lying in one bed together,
    And he just under us.
Buzzano.   In my fleabitten trundle bed.   70
Clerk. Peace, sirrah.
Henrico.   About midnight I awaking
    And this Buzzano too, my brother in his sleep
    Thus cried out, 'oh, 'twas I that murdered him;
    This hand that killed him.'
Gyron.   Heard you this, sirrah?
Buzzano. As sure as I hear you now.   75
Alquevezzes. And you'll be sworn 'twas he that so cried out?
Buzzano. If I were going to be hanged, I'd swear.
Clerk. Forbear the court.   *Exit* BUZZANO.
Macada. All this is but presumption. If this be all
    The shot you make against him, your bullets stick   80
    In a mud wall, or if they meet resistance,
    They back rebound and fly in your own face.
Medina. Bring your best forces up, for these are weak ones.
Henrico. Then here I throw my glove, and challenge him
    To make this good upon him; that at coming home   85
    He first told me my father died in France,
    Then, some hours after that, he was not dead,

80–1. *your bullets ... mud wall*] you do not cause injury to your target (i.e.
Manuell).

120   DICK OF DEVONSHIRE   [ACT 5

But that he left him in Lorraine at Nancy.
Then at Chaalons in Burgundy, and lastly,
He said to Don Fernando he was in Paris.   90
Fernando. He did indeed.
Macada.   What then?
Henrico. Then, when in's chamber we were going to bed,
He suddenly looked wild, catched me by the hands,
And falling on his knees, with a pale face
And troubled conscience, he confessed he killed him;   95
Nay, swore he basely murdered him.
Macada.   [*To Manuell*] What say you to this?
Alquevezzes. Now he comes close up to you.
Manuell.   He is my murderer,
For I am none, so let my innocence guard me.
I never spake with a distracted voice,
Ne'er fell to him, on my knees, spake of no father,   100
No murdered father. He's alive as I am,
And some foul devil stands at the fellow's elbow,
Jogging him to this mischief. The villain belies me,
And on my knees, my Lords, I beg that I
And my white innocence may tread that path   105
Beaten out before us by that man, my brother.
Command a case of rapiers to be sent for,
And let me meet his daring. I know him valiant,
But I am doubly armed, both with a courage
Fiery as his can be, and with a cause   110
That spits his accusation full in the face.
Macada. The combat in this case cannot be granted,
And here's the reason. When a man accuses
A friend, much more a brother, for a fact
So foul as murder (murder of a father),   115
The law leaps straight way to the challenger,
To take his part. Say he that doth accuse
Should be decrepit, lame and weak, or sickly,
The other strong and lusty; think you a kingdom
Will hazard so a subject, when the quarrel   120
Is for a kingdom's right? If y'are so valiant,
You then must call the law into the field,

---

120. *hazard so a subject*] put the challenger at risk.

| SC I] | DICK OF DEVONSHIRE | 121 |

But not the man.
Manuell.   I have done. Let law proceed.
Macada. This cannot serve your turn. Say he does belie
                                              you;
   He stakes against your body his own soul.   125
   Say there is no such murder, yet the law
   Fastens on you; for any man accused
   For killing of his father may be racked
   To draw confession from him. Will you confess?
Manuell. I cannot, must not, will not.   130
Macada. Jailer, take and prepare him for the rack.
   We'll see it done here.
Henrico.   You are righteous judges.
Manuell. Oh villain, villain, villain.   *Exit with the* JAILER.
Medina. Where's the wronged lady?
Alquevezzes.   Stand you still at the bar.
   You are now another man, sir; your scale turns.   135

      FERNANDO *fetches in* ELEONORA.

Macada. Look on the prisoner. Do you know him, Lady?
Eleonora. Would I had ne'er had cause to say I know him!
Macada. Of what do you accuse him?
Eleonora.   As the murderer
   Both of my name and honour. In the hurry,
   When the city (they said) was ready to be taken,   140
   I being betrothed to this young gentleman,
   My father brought me to his father's house,
   Telling me there dwelt safety. There dwelt villainy,
   Treason, lust, baseness; for this godless man
   (The storm being o'er) came in and forced from me   145
   The jewel of my virgin honour.
Henrico.   False.
Fernando. I would not have thee think (thou graceless wretch)
   She, being contracted to thee, loving thee,

---

137. him!] *Malone (conj.); possibly* him? *Q.*

---

   134. *the wronged lady*] Eleonora.
   135. *your scale turns*] scales of Justice.
   147–52. *I would ... true*] I do not want you to think that Eleonora would put her own honour and reputation, and mine and that of my house, at risk by making the claim of rape publicly if it were not completely true.

122 DICK OF DEVONSHIRE [ACT 5

Loving thee far more dearly than herself,
Would wound her virtue so, so blot her fame, 150
And bring a scandal on my house and me,
Were not the fact most true.
Henrico. Most false, by all that ever man can swear by.
We falling out, I told her once I ne'er
Would marry her, and so she works this mischief. 155
Gyron. You here stand charged for ravishing her,
and you must marry her, or she may have your life.
Macada. Lady, what say you? Which had you rather have?
His life or him?
Eleonora. I am not cruel. Pay me my first bond
of marriage, which you sealed to, and I free you, 160
and shall with joy run flying to your arms.
Alquevezzes. Law you?
Macada.   That's easy enough.
Henrico. Racks, gibbets, wheels make sausages of my flesh
first;
I'll be tied to no man's strumpet.
Alquevezzes. Then you must look to die.
Macada.   Lady, withdraw. 165
Henrico. Well if I do, somebody shall pack.
Eleonora. Oh me, unfortunate creature!   *Exit.*

Enter MANUELL *to be racked;* JAILER, *and* OFFICERS.

Medina. Don Manuell Gusman, ere you taste the tortures
Which you are sure to feel, will you confess
This murder of your father? 170
Manuell. Pray give me privacy a little with my brother.
All.   Take it.
Manuell. O brother, your own conscience knows you wrong
me.
I'll rather suffer on the gallow tree
Than thus be torn in pieces; canst thou see me
Thus worried amongst hangmen? Dear Henrico, 175
For Heaven's sake, for thine own sake pity me.

---

158. *His life or him?*] Would you prefer to see him executed or marry him?
162. *Law you?*] Is that permissible by law?
166. *pack*] influence the jury.
174. *torn in pieces*] i.e. torn apart on the rack.

SC 1]   DICK OF DEVONSHIRE   123

All. What says he?
Henrico.   Cunning, cunning, cunning traitor!
    In my ear he confesses all again, and prays me
    To speak to you.
Macada.   Will you openly confess?
Manuell. No, no, I cannot. Caitiff, I spake not so.   180
    I must not wound my conscience, to lay on it
    A guilt it knows not. I'll not so dishonour
    My father, nor my ancestors before me,
    Nor my posterity, with such an earthquake
    To shake our noble house.
Macada.   Give him the law, then.   185
Manuell. I'll meet a thousand deaths first.
Henrico. Pluck, and pluck home, for he's a murderous villain.
Manuell. Thou worse, a devil.
Macada.   Rack him.
Manuell. Oh stay; for Heaven's sake spread your mercy.
    I do confess the murder. I killed my father.   190
All. Take him off.
Manuell.   This hand stabbed him.
Macada.   Where?
Manuell. Near St. Germains in Paris, in a dark night, and
                                    then I fled.
Macada. Thy own tongue is thy judge; take him away.
    Tomorrow look to die. Send him a confessor.
Jailer. I'll have a holy care of him.   195
                    Exit MANUELL, *led by the* JAILER.
Henrico. Who's now, my lords, the villain?

                    Enter ELEONORA *and* BUZZANO.

Eleonora. Oh Justice, here's a witness of my rape.
Macada. Did you see't sirrah?
Buzzano.   See't? No, sir; would I had.
    But when she was in labour, I heard her cry out, 'help,
    help', and the gambol being ended, she came in like a   200
    mad woman, ruffled and crumpled, her hair about her

---

    194. *Send him a confessor*] Cf. the Friars who visited Pike in his cell. This
becomes important for the disguise adopted by Don Pedro later in the scene.
    198. *would I had*] if only I had.
    199. *in labour*] in distress, i.e. during the rape.

124 DICK OF DEVONSHIRE [ACT 5

ears; and he all unbraced, sweating as if he had been
thrashing. And afterwards he told me, my Lords, that he
had down-diddled her.

Henrico. I now am lost indeed, and on my knee 205
 Beg pardon of that goodness, that pure temple
 Which my base lust prophaned; and will make good
 My wrongs to her by marriage.

Macada.   What say you, Lady?

Eleonora. He spurned my mercy when it flew to him
 And courted him to kiss it; therefore now 210
 I'll have his life.

Fernando.   That life, so had, redeems
 Thine and thy father's infamy. Justice, my Lords.

Henrico. Cruel creature.

Macada.   Take him away, and lead him to his brother.
 You both must die next morning.

Henrico.   I deserve it,
 And so that slave too, that betrayed his master. 215

Buzzano. Why should not I betray my master, when he
 betrayed his mistress?

Clerk. Get you gone, sirrah.

        Exeunt HENRICO *&* BUZZANO.

Macada.   You are dismissed, fair Lady.
 You shall have law; your ravisher shall die.

Eleonora. Oh that my life from death could set him free!

           Exit.

Macada. Pray, Don Fernando, follow her, and soften 220
 Her heart to pity the poor gentleman.
 The crime is not so capital.

Fernando.   I'll do my best.   *Exit.*

Macada. That such a noble Spaniard as Don Pedro
 Should be so cursed in's children!

---

 209. *when it flew to him*] when I offered it.

 215. *that slave too*] Buzzano.

 219. *that ... free*] This line is incongruous in the scene. Eleonora had the
opportunity to free Henrico, but opted for his execution following his earlier
rejection of her mercy. This line sits uncomfortably, therefore, against line
211, above.

 222. *The crime is not so capital*] The crime is not so severe as to warrant
a death sentence.

SC I]   DICK OF DEVONSHIRE   125

Enter BUZZANO, DON PEDRO, FERNANDO
and ELEONORA.

Buzzano. He's come, he's come. My Lord, Don Pedro   225
    Gusman, is still alive. See, see.
Macada. Let us descend to meet a happiness crowns all our
    expectations.
Don Pedro. Whilst I meet a thunder strikes me dead.
    Oh poor, wronged lady.   230
    The poison, which the villain pours on thy honour,
    Runs more into my veins than all the venom
    He spits at me, or my dear boy, his brother.
    My Lords, your pardon, that I am transported
    With shame and sorrow thus beyond myself,   235
    Not paying to you my duty.
All.   Your love, Don Pedro.
Macada. Conceal yourself a while. Your sons we'll send for,
    And show them death's face presently.
Don Pedro.   I'll play a part in't.
                                      Exit.
Macada. Let them be fetched, and speak not of a father.
Teniente. This shall be done.   *Exit.*
Macada.   Is your compassion, Lady, yet awake?   240
    Remember that the scaffold, hangman, sword,
    And all the instruments death plays upon,
    Are hither called by you; 'tis you may stay them.
    When at the bar there stood your ravisher
    You would have saved him, then you made your choice   245
    To marry him. Will you then kill your husband?
Eleonora. Why did that husband then rather choose death
    Than me to be his bride? Is his life mine?
    Why then, because the law makes me his judge,
    I'll be, like you, not cruel, but reprieve him.   250
    My prisoner shall kiss mercy.
Macada.   Y'are a good lady.
Medina. Lady, until they come, repose yourself.
                                Exit ELEONORA.

---

  227. *crowns*] exceeds.
  236. *Not paying to you my duty*] not recognising your noble status.
  238. *death's face*] the face of a dead man (i.e. Don Pedro).
  243. *stay them*] stop them; call them off.

126   DICK OF DEVONSHIRE   [ACT 5

Enter PIKE *and a* GENTLEMAN *with letters.*

Macada. How now? So soon come back? Why thus returned?
Gentleman. Our journey to Madrid the King himself
     Cuts off by these, his royal letters, sent   255
     Upon the wings of speed to all your Graces.
     He lay one night since at your house, my Lord,
     Where, by your noble wife, he had a welcome
     Fitting his greatness, and your will.
Alquevezzes.   I'm glad of 't.
Macada. The King, our master, writes here, Englishman,   260
     He has lost a subject by you, yet refers
     Himself to us about you.
Pike.   Again, I stand here
     To lay my own life down, please his high Majesty
     To take it, for what's lost, his fate to fall
     Was *fortune de la guerre*; and at the feet   265
     Of his most royal Majesty, and at yours
     (My princely Lords and Judges), low as th'earth,
     I throw my wretched self, and beg his mercy.
Macada. Stand up. That mercy, which you ask, is signed by
     our most royal master.   270
Pike. My thanks to Heaven, him, and your Graces.
Macada. The King further writes here,
     That though your nation came in thunder hither,
     Yet he holds out to you his enemy
     Two friendly proffers; serve him in his dominions
     Either by land or sea, and thou shalt live   275
     Upon a golden pension, such a harvest
     As thou ne'er reapst in England.
Pike.   His kingly favours
     Swell up in such high heaps above my merit,
     Could I rear up a thousand lives, they cannot
     Reach half the way. I'm his, to be his vassal,   280
     His galley slave, please you to chain me to the oar.
     But with his highness' pardon and your allowance,

261–2. *refers ... about you*] has trusted our favourable account of you.
265. *de la guerre*] of war.

sc i]   DICK OF DEVONSHIRE   127

I beg one boon.
All.   What is't?
Pike.   That I may once more
    See my own country chimneys cast out smoke,
    And service to my King, (The King of England)   285
    Let me pay that bond I owe my life
    Of my allegiance. And that being paid,
    There is another obligation; one,
    To a woeful wife, and wretched children,
    Made wretched by my misery. I therefore beg,   290
    Entreat, implore, submissively hold up my hands,
    To have his kingly pity, and yours, to let me go.
Alquevezzes. Let him e'en go.
Macada.   Well, since we cannot win you to our service,
    We will not wean you from your country's love.
    The King, our Lord, commands us here to give you   295
    A hundred pistoletts to bear you home.
Pike. A royal bounty, which my memory
    Shall never lose, no, nor these noble favours
    Which from the Lady Marquesse Alquevezzes
    Rained plenteously on me.
Alquevezzes.   What did she to thee?   300
Gyron. How did she entertain thee?
Pike. Rarely, it is a brave, bounteous, munificent, magnificent
    Marquezza. The great Turk cannot taste better meat than
    I have eaten at this lady's table.
Alquevezzes. So, so.   305
Pike. And for a lodging; if the curtains about my bed had been
    cut of sunbeams, I could not lie in a more glorious
    chamber.
Macada. You have something then to speak of our women
    when y'are in England.   310
Pike. This box, with a gold chain in't for my wife, and some
    pretty things for my children, given me by your honoured
    Lady would else cry out on me. There's a Spanish shirt,
    richly laced and seamed, her gift too, and whosoever lays

---

283. *boon*] request.
313. *cry out on me*] call me out as a liar.

128   DICK OF DEVONSHIRE   [ACT 5

a foul hand upon her linen in scorn of her bounty, were   315
as good flay the devil's skin over his ears.

Macada. Well said. In England thou wilt drink her health?

Pike. Were it a glass as deep to the bottom as a Spanish pike
is long, an Englishman shall do't; her health and Don
John's wife's too.   320

Enter JAILER.

Jailer. The prisoners are upon coming.

Macada. Stand by, Englishman.

Enter TENIENTE, HENRICO, MANUELL,
DON PEDRO *(as a friar).*

At another door ELEONORA.

Macada. Give the lady room there!

Clerk.   Peace!

Macada. Your facts are both so foul, your hated lives
Cannot be too soon shortened. Therefore these Lords   325
Hold it not fit to lend you breath till morning,
But now to cut you off.

Both.   The stroke is welcome.

Don Pedro. Shall I prepare you?

Henrico.   Save your pains, good father.

Manuell. We have already cast up our accounts
And sent, we hope, our debts up into Heaven.   330

Fernando. Our sorrows, and our sighs fly after them.

Don Pedro. Then your confession of the murder stands
As you yourself did set it down?

Manuell.   It does.
But on my knees I beg, this marginal note
May stick upon the paper; that no guilt,   335
But fear of tortures frighted me to take
That horrid sin upon me. I am as innocent
And free as are the stars from plotting treason

---

324. *Your facts*] the facts about what you have done (i.e. Manuell's murder
of his father and Henrico's rape of Eleonora).

327. *now to cut you off*] execute you now.

stroke] of the executioner's axe.

335–7. *no guilt … upon me*] I confessed because I was scared of being
tortured, not because I was guilty of the crime of which I was accused.

SC I]   DICK OF DEVONSHIRE   129

'Gainst their first mover.
Don Pedro.   I was then in France,
   When of your father's murder, the report   340
   Did fill all Paris.
Manuell.   Such a reverend habit
   Should not give harbour to so black a falsehood.
Henrico. 'Tis black, and of my dying; for 'twas I,
   To cheat my brother of my father's lands,
   Laid this most hellish plot.   345
Fernando. For three hellish sins, robbery, rape and murder.
Henrico. I'm guilty of all three. His soul's as white
   And clear from murder as this holy man
   From killing me.
Don Pedro.   No, there's a thing about me
   Shall strike thee into dust, and make thy tongue   350
   With trembling to proclaim thyself a villain,
   More than thou yet hast done; see, 'tis my eye.
Henrico. Oh, I am confounded!

                    HENRICO *falls.*

Manuell.   But I comforted,
   With the most Heavenly apparition
   Of my dear honoured father.
Fernando.   Take thou comfort   355
   By two more apparitions, of a father,
   And a lost daughter, yet here found for thee.
Manuell. Oh noble sir, I pray forgive my brother.
Eleonora. See sir, I do; and with my hand reach to him
   My heart to give him new life.
Fernando.   Rise, my Henrico!   360
Macada. Rise, and receive a noble-minded wife
   Worth troupes of other women.
Henrico.   Shame leaves me speechless.
Don Pedro. Get thee a tongue again, and pray and mend.

   341–2. *Such … falsehood*] The portrayal of immorality concealed beneath
a holy garment was a common motif in early modern drama. Compare the
Fat Bishop in Middleton's *A Game at Chess* (1625).
   343. *of my dying*] I dyed it black, i.e. corrupted it.
   352. *'tis my eye*] Don Pedro reveals his true identity.
   353. *confounded*] shamed.

130   DICK OF DEVONSHIRE   [ACT 5

Macada. Letters shall forthwith fly into Madrid
    To tell the King these stories of two brothers,   365
    Worthy the courtiers' reading. Lovers, take hands.
    Hymen and gentle faeries strew your way;
    Our Sessions turns into a bridal day.
All. Fare thee well, Englishman.
Pike.   I will ring peals
    Of prayers of you all my Lords, and noble Dons.   370
Macada. Do so, if thou hast just cause. Howsoever,
    When thy swift ship cuts through the curlèd main,
    Dance to see England, yet speak well of Spain.
Pike. I shall. Where must I leave my pistoletts?
Gentleman. Follow me.   375

                    Exeunt omnes.

          Finis.

---

367. *Hymen*] In Greek and Roman mythology, the god of marriage.

APPENDIX 1
Transcription of Richard Peeke's *Three to One*

Three to One. Being, An English-Spanish Combat, Performed by a Western Gentleman, of Tavistock in Devonshire with an English Quarterstaff, against Three Spanish Rapiers and Poniards, at Sherries in Spain, The fifteen day of November, 1625.

In the Presence of Dukes, Counts Marquesses, and other Great Dons of Spain, being the Council of War.

The Author of this Book, and Actor in this Encounter, Richard Peeke.

TO THE KINGS MOST EXCELLENT Majesty

Gracious Sovereign,

If I were again in Spain, I should think no happiness on Earth, so great, as to come into England, and at your royal feet, lay down the story of my dangers, and peregrination; which I tell, as a late sea-wrackt man, (toss'd and beaten with many misfortunes;) yet, setting my weary body at last on a blessed shore. my hands now lay hold upon your altar, which is to me a Sanctuary. here I am safe in harbour.

That Psalm of Kingly David, which I sung in my Spanish Captivity, *(When as we sat in Babylon, &c.)* I now have changed to another tune; saying, (with the same Prophet, *Great is thy Mercy towards me (O Lord,) for thou hast delivered my soul from the lowest grave.* And, as your Majesty hath been graciously pleased, both to let your poor soldier and subject, behold your royal person, and to hear him speak in his rude language; So, if your Majesty, vouchsafe to cast a princely eye on these his unhandsome papers; new sunbeams shall spread over him, and put a quickening soul into that bosom, which otherwise must want life, for want of your comfort. Those graces, from your excellent clemency, (already received) being such, that I am ashamed, and sorry, not to have endur'd, and to have done more in foreign countries, for the honour of yours; when from so high a throne, my sovereign deigns to look down, on a creature so unworthy, whose life, he prostrates before your Highness.

132   APPENDICES

Ever resting, Your Majesty's most Humble and Loyal Subject, Richard Peeke.

Three to One. Being, An *English-Spanish* Combat

Loving Countrymen; Not to weary you with long preambles, unnecessary for you to read, and troublesome for me to set down; I will come roundly to the matter; entreating you, not to cast a malicious eye upon my actions, nor rashly to condemn them, or to stagger in your Opinions of my performance, sithence I am ready with my life to justify what I set down; the truth of this relation being warranted by noble proofs, and testimonies not to be questioned.

I am a Western man, Devonshire my country, and Tavistock my place of habitation.

I know not what the court of a King means, nor what the fine phrases of silken courtiers are. a good ship I know, and a poor cabin, and the language of a cannon and therefore, as my breeding has been rough, (scorning delicacy) and my present being consisteth altogether upon the soldier, (blunt, plain, and unpolished;) so must my writings be, proceeding from fingers fitter for the pike than the pen. and so (kind countrymen) I pray receive them. Neither ought you to expect better from me, because I am but the chronicler of my own story.

After I had seen the beginning and end of *Argeires* voyage, I came home, somewhat more acquainted with the world, but little amended in estate; my body more wasted and weather-beaten, but my purse never the fuller, nor my pockets thicker lined.

Then, the drum beating up for a new expedition, in which, many noble gentlemen, and heroical spirits, were to venture their honours, lives, and fortunes. cables could not hold me, for away I would, and along I vowed to go, and did so.

The design opening itself at sea for Cales, proud I was to be employed there, where so many gallants, and English worthies, did by their examples, encourage the common soldier to honourable darings.

The ship I went in, was called *The Convertine,* (one of the Navy Royal.) The Captain, Thomas Portar.

On the two and twentieth day of October, being Saturday, 1625, our fleet came into Cales, about three of the clock in the afternoon, we being in all, some hundred and ten sailors.

The Saturday-night, some sixteen sailors of the Hollanders, and about ten Whitehall-Men (who in England are called Colliers) were

APPENDICES 133

commanded to fight against the Castle of Puntal, standing three miles from Cales, who did so accordingly, and discharged (in that service) at the least one thousand six hundred shots.

On the Sunday morning following, the Earle of Essex going up very early, and an hour at least before us to the fight, commanded our ship (the *Convertine*, being of his squadron) to follow him: the castle playing hard and hotly upon his Lordship.

Captain Portar, and the Master of our ship, (whose name is M. Hill,) having upon sight of so fierce an encounter, an equal desire to do something worthy themselves, and their country, came up so close to the castle, as possibly men in such a danger either could, or durst adventure, and there fought bravely. the castle bestowing upon us a hot salutation (and well becoming our approach) with bullets; whose first shot killed three of our men, passing through and through our ship, the second killed four, and the third two more at least, with great spoil and battery to our ship. the last shot flying so close by Captain Portar, that with the wind of the bullet, his very hands had almost lost the sense of feeling, being struck into a sudden numbness.

Upon this, Captain Portar perceiving the danger we, and our ship were in, commanded a number of us to get upon the upper deck, and with our small shot to try if we could force the cannoneers from their ordnance.

We presently advanced ourselves, fell close to our work, and plied them with pellets; in which hot and dangerous Service, one Master William Jewell behaved himself both manly and like a noble soldier, expressing much valour, ability of body, and readiness; with whom, and some few more, I (amongst the rest) stood the brunt, which continued about three hours.

Our ship lay all this while with her starboard side to the Fort, who beating us continually, with at least two hundred muskets, whose bullets flew so thick, that our shrouds were torn in pieces, and our tacklings rent to nothing; and when she came off, there were to be seen five hundred bullets (at the least) sticking in her side. I, for my part (without vain glory be it spoken) discharging at this time, some threescore and ten shot, as they recounted to me who charged my pieces for me.

In the heat of this fight, Sir William Sentliger (whether called up by my Lord of Essex, or coming of himself, I know not) seeing us so hardly beset, and that we had but few shot upon our deck, in regard of the enemies number, which played upon us, came with a valiant and noble resolution, out of another ship into ours, bringing

134 APPENDICES

some forty soldiers with him, who there with us, renewed a second fight, as hot, or hotter than the former. where in this fight, one of our bullets was shot into the mouth of a Spanish cannon, where it sticketh fast, and putteth that roarer to silence.

Upon this bravery, they of the Fort began to wax calmer, and cooler. and in the end, most part of their gunners being slain, gave over shooting, but yielded not the fort until night.

Whilst this skirmish continued, a company of Spaniards within the castle, by the advantage of a wall, whose end jutting out, they still as they discharged, retired behind it, saving themselves, and extremely annoying us; I removed into the fore-castle of our ship, and so plied them with hail-shot, that they forsook their stand.

What men on our part were lost (by their small shot) I cannot well remember, but sure I am, not very many. Yet the Spaniards afterwards, before the Governor of Cales, confessed they lost about fifty, whose muskets they cast into a well, because our men should not use them, throwing the dead bodies in after.

My hurts and bruises here received, albeit they were neither many, nor dangerous, yet were they such, that when the fight was done, many gentlemen in our ship for my encouragement, gave me money.

During this battle, the Hollanders and White-Hall-Men, you must think, were not idle, for their great pieces went off continually, from such of their ships as could conveniently discharge, because our ship lay between them and the Fort; and they so closely plied their work, that at this battery were discharged from the ordnance, at least four thousand bullets.

The castle being thus quieted, (though as yet not yielded) the Earl of Essex, about twelve at noon, landed his regiment close by the Fort, the Spaniards looking over the walls to behold them. upon sight of which, many of those within the castle (to the number of six score) ran away; we pursuing them with shouts, hollerings, and loud noises, and now and then a piece of ordnance overtook some of the Spanish hares, and stayed them from running farther.

Part of our men being thus landed, they marched up not above a flight shot off, and there rested themselves. Then about six at night the castle yielded, upon composition, to depart with their arms, and colours flying, and no man to offend them; which was performed accordingly.

The Captain of the Fort, his name was Don Francisco Busta-mante, who presently upon the delivery, was carried aboard the

APPENDICES 135

Lord General's ship, where he had a soldierly welcome; and the next day, he, and all his company were put over to Port Real, upon the mainland because they should not go to Cales, which is an island.

Monday. October 24. On the Monday, having begun early in the morning, all our forces, about no-one were landed, and presently marched up to a bridge, between Puntal and Cales; in going up to which, some of our men were unfortunately and unmanly surprised, and before they knew their own danger, had there their throats cut; some having their brains beaten out with the stocks of muskets; others, their noses sliced off; whilst some heads were spurned up and down the streets like footballs, and some ears worn in scorn in Spanish hats. for when I was in prison in Cales, (whether some of these Spanish picaroes were brought in for flying from the castle), I was an eye witness, of English men's ears worn in that despiteful manner.

What the forces being on shore did, or how far they went up, I cannot tell, for I was no Land-Soldier, and therefore all that while kept aboard. yet about twelve of the clock, when they were marched out of sight, I (knowing that other English men had done the like the very same day,) ventured on shore likewise, to refresh myself, with my sword only by my side, because, I thought the late storms had beaten all the Spaniards in, and therefore feared no danger.

On, therefore, I softly walked, viewing the desolation of such a place, for I saw nobody. yet far had I not gone from the shore, but some English men were come even almost to our ships, and from certain gardens had brought with them many oranges and lemons.

The sight of these, sharpened my stomach the more to go on, because I had a desire to present some of those fruits to my Captain. Hereupon, I demanded of them, what danger there was in going? They said, None, but that all was husht, and not a Spaniard stirring.

We parted, they to the ships, I forward. and before I had reached a mile, I found (for all their talking, of no danger) three Englishmen stark dead, being slain, lying in the way, it being full of deep sandy pits, so that I could hardly find the passage, and one, some small distance from them, not fully dead.

The groans which he uttered, led me to him; and finding him lying on his belly, I called to him, and turning him on his back, saw his wounds, and said; Brother, what villain has done this mischief to thee? He lamented in sighs and doleful looks, and casting up his eyes to Heaven, but could not speak. I then resolved (and was about it) for Christian charity's sake; and for Countries sake, to have

136 APPENDICES

carried him on my back to our ships, far off though they lay, and there (if by any possible means it could have been done,) to have recovered him.

But my good intents were prevented; for on a sudden, came rushing in upon me, a Spanish horseman, whose name, as afterward I was informed, was Don Juan of Cales, a Knight; I seeing him make speedily and fiercely at me, with his drawn weapon, suddenly whip'd out mine, wrapping my cloak about mine arm. five or six skirmishes we had, and for a pretty while, fought off and on.

At last, I getting with much ado, to the top of a sandy hillock, the horseman nimbly followed up after; by good fortune to me, (though bad to himself) he had no petronel or pistols about him; and therefore clapping spurs to his horse sides, his intent, as it seemed, was, with full career to ride over me, and trample me under his horse's feet. but a Providence greater than his fury, was my guard.

Time was it for me to look about warily, and to lay about lustily, to defend a poor life so hardly distressed. as therefore his horse was violently breaking in upon me, I struck him into the eyes, with a flap of my cloak; upon which, turning sideward, I took my advantage, and as readily as I could, stepping in, it pleased God, that I should pluck my enemy down, and have him at my mercy, for life, which notwithstanding, I gave him; he falling on his knees, and crying out in French to me. *Pardone moy le vous pree, le suis un buon Chrestien.* Pardon me Sir, I am a good Christian.

I, seeing him brave, and having a soldier's mind to rifle him, I searched for jewels, but found, only five Pieces of Eight about him, in all amounting to twenty shillings English. yet he had gold, but that I could not come by; for, I was in haste to have sent his Spanish Knighthood home on foot, and to have taught his horse an English pace.

Thus far, my voyage for oranges sped well, but in the end, proved sour sauce to me. And it is harder to keep a victory, than to obtain; so, here it fell out with mine. For, fourteen Spanish musketeers, spying me so busy about one of their countrymen, bent all the mouths of their pieces to kill me, which they could not well do, without endangering this Don John's life; so that I was enforced (and glad I scap'd so too) to yield myself their prisoner.

True Valour (I see) goes not always in good clothes; for, he whom before I had surprised, seeing me fast in the snare, and (as the event proved) disdaining that his countrymen should report him so dishonoured, most basely, (when my hands were in a manner bound

APPENDICES 137

behind me) drew out his weapon, (which the rest had taken from me, to give him) and wounded me through the face, from ear to ear, and had there killed me, had not the fourteen musketeers rescued me from his rage.

Upon this, I was led in triumph, into the town of Cales. an owl not more wondered and hooted at, a dog not more cursed.

In my being led thus along the streets, A Flemming spying me, cried out aloud; whither do you lead this English dog? Kill him, kill him, he's no Christian. And with that, breaking through the crowd, in upon those who held me, ran me into the body with a halberd, at the reins of my back, at the least four inches.

One Don Fernando, an ancient gentleman, was sent down this summer, from the King at Madrill, with soldiers; but before our fleet came, the soldiers were discharged; they of Cales, never suspecting that we meant to put in there.

Before him, was I brought to be examined, yet few, or no questions at all, were demanded of me because, he saw I was all bloody in my clothes, and so wounded in my face and jaws, that I could hardly speak. I was therefore committed presently to prison, where I lay eighteen days. The noble gentleman, giving express charge, that the best surgeons should be sent for, least, being so basely hurt and handled by cowards, I should be demanded at his hands.

I being thus taken on the Monday, when I went on shore, the fleet departed the Friday following, from Cales, at the same time when I was there a prisoner.

Yet, thus honestly was I used by my worthy friend Captain Portar; he above my deserving, complaining, that he feared he had lost such a man. My Lord General (by the solicitation of Master John Glanville, Secretary to the Fleet) sent three men on shore, to enquire in Cales for me, and to offer (if I were taken) any reasonable ransom. but the town, thinking me a better prize than (indeed) I was, denied me, and would not part from me.

Then came a command to the Teniente, or Governor of Cales, to have me sent to Sherrys, (otherwise called Xerez,) lying three leagues from Cales. Wondrous unwilling (could I otherwise have chosen) was I to go to Sherry, because, I feared I should then be put to Tortures.

Having therefore a young man, (an Englishman, and a merchant, whose name was Goodrow,) my fellow prisoner, who lay there for debt. and so I thinking there was no way with me but one; (That I must be sent packing to my long home,) thus I spake unto him.

138 APPENDICES

Countryman, what my name is, our partnership in misery hath made you know; And with it, know that I am a Devonshire man born, and Tavistock the place of my once-abiding. I beseech you, if God ever send you liberty, and that you sail into England, take that country in your way; commend me to my wife and children, made wretched by me, an unfortunate father, and husband. tell them, and my friends, (I entreat you, for God's cause) that if I be (as I suspect I shall be) put to death in Sherris, I will die a Christian soldier, no way, I hope, dishonouring my King, country, or the justice of my cause, or my religion.

Anon after, away was I conveyed with a strong guard, by the Governor of Cales, and brought into Sherrys on a Thursday, about twelve at night.

On the Sunday following, two Friars were sent to me, (both of them being Irishmen, and speaking very good English; one of them was called Padre Juan, (Father John.) After a sad and grave salutation; Brother (quoth he) I come in love to you, and charity to your soul, to confess you. And if to us, (as your spiritual ghostly fathers) you will lay open your sins, we will forgive them, and make your way to Heaven, for tomorrow you must die.

I desired them, that they would give me a little respite, that I might retire into a private chamber, and instantly I would repair to them, and give them satisfaction. Leave I had; away I went, and immediately returned. They asked me, if I had yet resolved, and whether I would come to confession. I told them, I had been at confession already. One of them demanded, with whom? I answered, with God the Father. And with nobody else (said the other?) Yes, (quoth I) and with Jesus Christ, my Redeemer, who hath both power and will, to forgive all men their sins, that truly repent; before these two, have I fallen on my knees, and confessed my grievous offences, and trust, they will give me a free absolution, and pardon.

What think you of the Pope? said Father John. I answered, I knew him not. They, hereupon, shaking their heads, told me, they were sorry for me, and so departed.

Whilst thus I lay in Sherrys, the captain of the fort (Don Francisco Bustamente) was brought in, prisoner for his life, because he delivered up the castle; but whether he died for it, or no, I cannot tell.

My day of trial being come, I was brought from prison, into the town of *Sherrys*, by two drums, and a hundred shot, before three

APPENDICES   139

Dukes, four Counts, or Earls, four Marquesses, besides other great
persons; the town having in it, at least, five thousand soldiers.

At my first appearing before the Lords, my sword lying before
them on a table, the Duke of Medina asked me if I knew that
weapon; it was reached to me; I took it, and embraced it in mine
arms, and with tears in mine eyes, kissed the pomel of it. He then
demanded, how many men I had killed with that weapon? I told
him, if I had killed one, I had not been there now, before that
princely assembly, for when I had him at my foot, begging for mercy,
I gave him life, yet he, then very poorly, did me a mischief. Then
they asked Don John (my prisoner) what wounds I gave him; he
said, none. Upon this he was rebuked, and told; that if upon our
first encounter, he had run me through, it had been a fair and noble
triumph; but so to wound me, being in the hands of others, they
held it base.

Then said the Duke of Medina to me; Come on English-Man,
What ship came you in? I told him, *The Convertine*. Who was your
Captain? Captaine Portar. What ordnance carried your ship? I said,
forty pieces. But the Lords looking all this while on a paper, which
they held in their hands. Duke Medina said, In their note, there was
but thirty eight.

In that paper (as after I was informed, by my two Irish interpret-
ers) there was set down, the number of our ships, their burden, men,
munition, victuall, captains, &c. as perfect, as we our selves had them
in England.

Of what strength (quoth another Duke) is the Fort at Plymouth?
I answered, very strong. What ordnance in it? Fifty said I. That is
not so, said he, there is but seventeen. How many soldiers are in the
Fort? I answered, two hundred. That is not so, (quoth a Count) there
is but twenty.

Marquesse Alquenezes asked me, Of what strength the little
Island was before Plymouth? I told him, I knew not. Then (quoth
he) we do.

Is Plymouth a walled town? Yes my Lords. And a good wall? Yes
said I, a very good wall. True, said a Duke, to leap over with a staff.
And hath the town, said the Duke of Medina, strong gates? Yes. But,
quoth he, there was neither wood nor iron to those gates, but two
days before your fleet came away.

Now, before I go any farther, let me not forget to tell you, that
my two Irish confessors, had been here in England the last summer,

APPENDICES

& when our fleet came from England, they came for Spain; having seen our King at Plymouth, when the soldiers there shewed their arms, and did then diligently observe what the King did, and how he carried himself.

How chance (said Duke Giron) did you not in all this bravery of the fleet take Cales, as you took Puntal? I replied, that the Lord General might easily have taken Cales, for he had near a thousand scaling ladders to set up, and a thousand men to loose; but he was loath to rob an almshouse, having a better market to go to. Cales, I told them, was held poor, unmanned, and unmunitioned. What better market, said Medina? I told him, Genoa, or Lisbon, and as I heard, there was instantly, upon this, an army of six thousand soldiers sent to Lisbon.

Then, quoth one of the Earls, when thou meetst me in Plymouth, wilt thou bid me welcome? I modestly told him, I could wish, they would not too hastily come to Plymouth, for they should find it another manner of place, then as now they sleight it.

Many other questions were put to me by these great Dons, which so well as God did enable me, I answered, they speaking in Spanish, and their words interpreted to me, by those two Irish men before spoken of, who also relate my several answers to the Lords.

And by the common people, who encompast me round, many jeerings, mockeries, scorns, and bitter jests, were to my face thrown upon our nation, which I durst not so much as bite my lip against, but with an inforced patient ear stood still, and let them run on in their railings.

At the length, amongst many other reproaches, and spiteful names, one of the Spaniards called English men Gallinas, (hens;) at which, the great Lords fell a laughing. Hereupon, one of the Dukes (pointing to the Spanish soldiers,) bid me note how their King kept them; and indeed, they were all wondrous brave in apparel, hats, bands, cuffs, garters, &c, and some of them in chains of gold. And asked farther, if I thought these would prove such hens as our English, when next year they should come into England? I said no. But being somewhat emboldened by his merry countenance, I told him as merrily, I thought they would be within one degree of hens. What meanst thou by that, said a Count? I replied, they would prove pullets, or chickens. Darest thou then (quoth Duke Medina, with a brow half angry) fight with one of these Spanish pullets.

O my Lord, said I, I am a prisoner, and my life at stake, and therefore dare not be so bold to adventure upon any such action.

APPENDICES   141

There were here of us English, some fourteen thousand, in which
number, there were above twelve thousand, better, and stouter men
then ever I shall be; yet, with the licence of this princely assembly,
I dare hazard the breaking of a rapier; and withall, told him, he was
unworthy the name of an English man, that should refuse to fight
with one man of any nation whatsoever. Hereupon, my shackles
were knocked off, and my iron ring and chain taken from my neck.

Room was made for the combatants, rapier and dagger the
weapons. A Spanish champion presents himself, named Signior
Tiago; when after we had played some reasonable good time, I
disarmed, him as thus.

I caught his rapier betwixt the bars of my poniard, and there held
it, till I closed in with him, and tripping up his heels, I took his
weapons out of his hands, and delivered them to the Dukes.

I could wish, that all you, my dear country-men, who read this
relation, had either been there, without danger, to have beheld us;
or, that he with whom I fought, were here in person, to justify the
issue of that combat.

I was then demanded, if I durst fight against another? I told them,
my heart was good to adventure; but humbly requested them, to
give me pardon, if I refused.

For, to myself I too well knew, that the Spaniard is haughty,
impatient of the least affront; and when he receives but a touch of
any dishonour, disgrace, or blemish, (especially in his own country,
and from an English man,) his revenge is implacable, mortal, and
bloody.

Yet being by the Noblemen, pressed again, and again, to try my
fortune with an other, I (seeing my life in the lion's paw, to struggle
with whom for safety, there was no way but one, and being afraid
to displease them,) said, that if their Graces, and Greatnesses, would
give me leave to play at mine own country weapon, called the
Quarter-Staff, I was then ready there, an opposite, against any
comer, whom they would call forth; and would willingly lay down
my life before those princes, to do them service; provided, my life
might by no foul means be taken from me.

Hereupon, the head of a halbert, which went with a screw, was
taken off, and the steal delivered to me; the other butt-end of the
staff having a short iron pike in it. This was my armour, and in my
place I stood, expecting an opponent.

At the last, a handsome and well spirited Spaniard steps forth,
with his rapier and poniard. They asked me, what I said to him? I

142 APPENDICES

told them, I had a sure friend in my hand, that never failed me, and therefore made little account of that one to play with, and should shew them no sport.

Then, a second (armed as before) presents himself. I demanded, if there would come no more? The Dukes asked, how many I desired? I told them, any number under six. Which resolution of mine, they smiling at, in a kind of scorn, held it not manly, (it seemed,) nor fit for their own honours, and glory of their nation, to worry one man with a multitude; and therefore appointed three only, (so weaponed) to enter into the lists.

Now Gentlemen, if here you condemn me, for plucking (with mine own hands) such an assured danger, upon mine own head; accept of these reasons for excuse.

To die, I thought it most certain, but to die basely, I would not. For three to kill one, had been to me no dishonour; to them (weapons considered,) no glory; an honourable subjection, I esteemed better, than an ignoble conquest. Upon these thoughts, I fell to it.

The rapier men traversed their ground, I, mine; tangerous Thrusts were put in, and with dangerous hazard avoided. Shouts echoed to Heaven, to encourage the Spaniards; not a shout, nor hand, to hearten the poore English man; only, Heaven I had in mine eye, the honour of my country in my heart, my fame at the stake, my life on a narrow bridge, and death both before me and behind me.

It was not now a time to dally, they still made full at me; and I had been a coward to myself, and a villain to my nation, if I had not called up all that weak manhood which was mine, to guard my own life, and overthrow my enemies.

Plucking up therefore a good heart, seeing myself faint and wearied, I vowed to my soul, to do something, ere she departed from me. And so setting all upon one cast, it was my good fortune (it was my God did it for me) with the butt-end where the iron pike was, to kill one of the three; and within a few bouts after, to disarm the other two, causing the one of them to fly into the army of soldiers then present, and the other for refuge fled behind the bench.

I hope, if the braving Spaniards set upon England (as they threaten,) we shall every one of us, give the repulse to more than three; of which good issue for the public, I take this my private success to be a pledge.

Now was I in greater danger, being (as I thought) in peace, than before, when I was in battle. For, a general murmur filled the air,

APPENDICES 143

with threatenings at me; the soldiers especially bit their thumbs, and how was it possible for me to scape?

Which, the Noble Duke of Medina Sidenia seeing, called me to him, and instantly caused proclamation to be made, that none, on pain of death, should meddle with me; and by his honorable protection, I got off; and not off, only with safety, but with money. For by the Dukes and Counts, were given me in gold, to the value of four pounds ten shillings sterling; and by the Marquesse Alquenezes himself, as much; he embracing me in his arms, and bestowing upon me, that long Spanish russet cloak I now wear, which he took from one of his men's backs; and withall, furnished me with a clean band and cuffs; it being one of the greatest favours, a Spanish Lord can do to a mean man, to reward him with some garment, as recompence of merit.

After our fight in Sherris, I was kept in the Marquesse Alquenezes's house, who one day (out of his noble affability) was pleasant in speech with me; and by my interpreter, desired I would sing. I willing to obey him (whose goodness I had tasted,) did so, and sung this Psalm. When as we sat in Babylon, &c. The meaning of which being told, he said to me, English man, comfort thy self, for thou art in no captivity.

After this, I was sent to the King of Spain, lying at Madrill; my conduct being four gentlemen of the Marquess Alquenezes; he allowing unto me, in the journey, twenty shillings a day when we travelled, and ten shillings a day when we lay still.

At my being in Madrill, before I saw the King; my entertainement (by the Marquesse Alquenezes's appointment,) was at his own house, where I was lodged in the most sumptuous bed that ever I beheld; and had from his noble Lady, a welcome far above my poor deserving but worthy the greatness of so excellent a woman; she bestowing upon me, whilst I lay in her house a very fair Spanish shirt, richly laced, and at my parting from Madrill, a chain of gold, and two jewels for my wife, and other pretty things for my children.

And now that her noble courtesies together, with my own thankfulness, lead me to speak of this honorable Spanish Lady; I might very justly be condemned of ingratitude, if I should not remember, with like acknowledgement, another rare pattern of feminine goodness, to me, a distressed, miserable stranger. And that was, the Lady of Don John of Cales; she, out of a respect she bare me, for saving her husband's life, came along with him to Sherrys, he being there to give in evidence against me; and as before, when I lay prisoner

144 APPENDICES

in Cales, so in Sherrys, she often relieved me with money, and other means; my duty and thanks ever wait upon them both.

Upon Christmas-day, I was presented to the King, the Queen, and Don Carolo the Infante. Being brought before him, I fell (as it was fit) on my knees. Many questions were demanded of me, which so well as my plain wit directed me, I resolved.

In the end, his Majesty offered me a yearly pension, (to a good value) if I would serve him, either at land or at sea; for which his royal favours, I confessing myself infinitely bound, and my life indebted to his mercy, most humbly intreated, that with his princely leave, I might be suffered to return into mine own country, being a subject only to the King of England, my Sovereign.

And besides that Bond of Allegiance, there was another obligation, due from me, to a wife and children; and therefore, most submissively beg'd, that his Majesty would be so princely minded, as to pity my estate, and to let me go. To which he at last granted; bestowing upon me, one hundred pistolets, to bear my charges.

Having thus left Spain, I took my way through some part of France; where, by occasion, happening into company of seven Spaniards, their tongues were too lavish in speeches against our nation; upon which, some high words flying up and down the room, I leaped from the table, and drew.

One of the Spaniards did the like (none of the rest being weaponed, which was more than I knew.)

Upon the noise of this bustling, two English men more came in, who understanding the abuses offered to our country, the Spaniards in a short time, recanted on their knees their rashness.

And so hoysing sail for England; I landed on the three and twenty day of April, 1626. at Fowey in Cornwall.

And thus endeth my Spanish Pilgrimage. With thanks to my good God, that in this extraordinany manner preserved me, amidst these desperate dangers.

Therefore most gracious God, (defender of men abroad, and protector of them at home,) how am I bounden to thy divine Majesty, for thy manifold mercies?

On my knees I thank thee, with my tongue I will praise thee, with my hands fight in thy quarrell, and all the days of my life serve thee.

Out of the Red Sea, I have escaped; from the lion's den, been delivered; I rescued from death, and snatched out of the jaws of destruction, only by thee, O my God; glory be to thy name, for ever, and ever. *Amen.*

APPENDICES 145

Certain Verses, Written by a Friend, in Commendations of the Author, *Richard Peeke*

Seldom do clouds so dim the day,
But Sol will once his beams display.
Though Neptune drives the surging seas,
Sometimes he gives them quiet ease;
And so few projects speed so ill,
But somewhat chanceth at our will.

I will not instance in the great,
Placed in honours higher seat;
Though virtue in a noble line
Comm[...]nds i[...], and the more doth shine.
Yet this is procu'd by sword and pen,
Desert oft dwells in private men.

My proof is not far hence to seek,
There is at hand brave Richard Peeke,
Whose worth his foes cannot revoke,
Born in the towne of Tavistock
In Devon, where Minerva sits
Shaping stout hearts, and pregnant wits.

This well resolu'd and hardy spark,
Aiming at fame, as at a mark,
Was not compell'd against his will,
In Mars his field to try his skill.
As voluntary he did go,
To serve his King against his foe.

If he had pleas'd, he might have spent
His days at home, in safe content.
But nursing valour in his breast,
He would adventure with the best,
Willing to shed his dearest blood,
To do his prince, and country good.

Thus bent, he adding wings to feet,
Departed with the English fleet.
There was no rub, nor stay at all,

The ships sailed with a pleasant gale.
In setting forth they by their hap,
Seem'd lul'd in Amphitrites lap.

At length they did arrive at Cales,
Where restless Peeke against the walls
Made fourescore shot towards the shore,
Making the Welkyn wide to roar.
He kept his standing in this strife,
Setting a straw by loss of life.

Into a vineyard afterward
He marcht, and stood upon his guard;
There he an horse-man did dismount,
By outward port of good account.
But did on him compassion take,
And spar'd his life for pity's sake.

The next assault, uneven he felt,
For with twelve Spaniards he dealt
At once, and held them lusty play,
Until through odds, theirs was the day.
From ear to ear they pearc'd his head,
And to the town him captive led.

In prison they him shut by night,
Loaden with chains of grievous weight,
All comfortless in dungeon deep,
Where stench annoys, and vermins creep.
He grovell'd in this loathsome cell,
Where ghastly frights and horrors dwell.

Yet nothing could his courage quail,
Hunger, nor thirst, nor wound, nor jail.
For being brought before a Don,
And askt, why England did set on
A scraping, not a pecking hen?
He answer'd, stain not English-men.

That England is a nation stout,
And till the last will fight it out.

APPENDICES 147

My selfe could prove by chivalry,
If for a captive this were free.
Why, (quoth the Duke) darst thou to fight
With any of my men in fight?

Of thousands whom in war you use,
Not one (quoth Peeke) do I refuse.
A chosen champion then there came,
Whose heels he tript, as at a game,
And from his hand his rapier took,
Presenting it unto the Duke.

Then three at once did him oppose,
They rapiers, he a long staff chose,
The use whereof so well he knows,
He conquered them with nimble blows.
One that beside him played his round,
He threw as dead unto the ground.

The noble Duke who this did see,
Commended Peeke, and set him free;
He gave him gifts, and did command
That none should wrong him in their land;
So well he did him entertain,
And sent him to the Court of Spain.

There he was fed with no worse meat,
Then which the King himself did eat;
His lodging rich, for he did lie
In furniture of tapestry.
The King what of him he had heard,
Did with his treasure well reward.

Our then ambassador was there,
Peeke's pike and praise he doth declare.
At Spanish Court whiles he attends,
He thrives for virtue's sake. As friends
Foes sent him in triumphant sort
Home from a foe and foreign port.

If thus his very foes him lov'd,
And deeds against themselves approv'd;

How should his friends his love embrace,
And yield him countenance and grace?
The praise and worth how can we cloke
Of manly Peeke of Tavistock?

FINIS.

J. D.

APPENDIX 2
Other documents relating to Richard Peeke

1 **Anon.,** *A true relation of a brave English strategem practised lately upon a sea-towne in Galizia, (one of the Kingdomes in Spaine) and most valiantly and succesfully performed by one English ship alone of 30. tonne, with no more than 35. men in her. As also, with two other remarkeable accidents betweene the English and Spaniards, to the glory of our nation* **(London: Mercurius Britannicus, 1626)**

In Lisbon not long since, a young Merchant (who for diverse respects desires to have his name concealed), being in the company of certain Dons, and falling in discourse about the value of several nations, they so far exceeded in the hyperbolies of their own praise, that they blusht not to affirm, that one Spaniard was able to beat two English men out of the field, which they in their braggadesme inforced so far, that though the rest were silent, thus young gentleman not able to conceal a true English spirit, after some retort of language there made a protestation. That if it pleased the Governor to give him leave, he himself would undertake, (making choice of his weapon) to fight singly against three of the proudest champions they would produce against him; to cut off circumstance, the challenge was accepted, the Governor prepared the combatants, with the time and place appointed: a great confluence of people assembled: where one young Merchant, armed only with his sword and Spanish pike in the lists appeared, who by the three adversaries was boldly and resolutely charged: but God and his good cause defended him so well, that the combat continued not long, and having received from them some few scratches, with the loss of a small quantity of blood, but without danger, he so actively and resolutely behaved himself against the survivors, that they after diverse wounds from him received begin to quail in their former courage, and fight more faintly and further off, which the Governor perceiving, commanded the combat to cease, and withall to guard him, the English man from the fury of the displeased multitude, who could have found in their

149

150 APPENDICES

hearts to have pluckt him in pieces, where calling him up to him conveyed him safe to his house, and after much commendation of his valour, very nobly secured him to his ship, wishing him for his own safety to be seen no more ashore, whose counsel he followed; and since with much envy from them, and great honour to us, he is arrived in his own country. (sigs. B2v–B3r)

2 *A brave warlike song containing a brief rehearsal of the deeds of chivalry, performed by the nine worthies of the world, the seven champions of Christendom, with many other remarkable warriors. To the tune of List lusty gallants*

Printer/Publisher for Fr Coules

1626?

Printed at London

The second Part. Containing other brave Warriors not ranckt among the Worthies, though as worthy.

To the same tune.

Cumberland and Essex,
Norris and brave Drake,
I'th raigne of Quéene Elizabeth
did many battels make.
Adventrous Martin Frobisher,
with Hawkins and some more,
From sea did bring great riches
unto our English shore.
Saint George, &c.

Bold Richard Pike of Tavistoke,
a towne in Devonshire,
Did combat with thrée Spaniards,
and came off fair and clear,
There's many other warriors,
whose names I will not tell.
Lest too prolix my Song should be,
and so, kind Friends, Farewell.
Saint George, &c.

APPENDICES   151

3 Letter from Dr Meddus to the Reverend Mead, 19 May 1626

Yesterday being Holy Thursday, one Pyke, a common soldier, left
behind the fleet at Cadiz, delivered a challenge to the Duke of
Buckingham from the Marquis of . . ., brother-in-law to the Conde
d'Olivares, in defence of the honour of his sister; affirming, moreover, that he had wronged Olivares, the King of Spain, and the King
of England, and therefore he would fight with him in any part of
France. This Pyke, a Devonshire man, being presented prisoner to
the Duke of Medina, he would needs have him fight at rapier or
dagger with a Spaniard, supposing he would not stand him two
thrusts; but Pyke, by a dexterous sleight, presently disarmed the
Spaniard of his rapier, without hurting him, and presented it to the
duke. He then offered with a quarterstaff to fight with three rapier
men, all which he vanquished and disarmed. Whereupon the duke
and marquis showed him much respect, and gave him money in
his purse; and the marquis carried him along with him to the court
of Madrid, where he presented him to the king, who invited him
to his service, and was answered, he would serve no king but his
own. So the king gave him fifty double ducats, and a safe conduct,
and sent him home. (Birch, 104. The ellipsis originates in Birch's
transcription.)

4 A Panegyrick Poem, or Tavistock's Enconium, composed by a Tavistock schoolmaster, Long, towards the end of Charles II's reign

Get also 'mongst Great Mars his thundering crew,
And all his warlike champions overview,
Search whether can be found again the like
For noble prowess to our Tav'stock Pike,
In whose renowned, never-dying, name,
Live England's honour, and the Spaniard's shame.
(Mrs Bray, *Traditions, Legends, Superstitions and Sketches of Devonshire
on the Borders of the Tamar and the Tavy*, vol. 3 [London: John Murray,
1879])

Further reading

PRE-1700 ITEMS

Manuscripts
Beinecke MS Osborn b.197, *Upon the English fleete sett forth. Anno. 1625*
British Library MS Egerton 1994, Anon., *Dick of Devonshire*
British Library MS Harley 6383, *A libell of Cales vyage 162* [*sic*]

Other printed items
Anon., *A True Relation of a Brave English Strategem Practised Lately Upon a Sea-Towne in Galizia (One of the Kingdomes in Spaine) and Most Valiantly and Succesfully Performed by One English Ship Alone of 30. Tonne, with No More Than 35. Men in Her. As Also, with Two Other Remarkeable Accidents Betweene the English and Spaniards, to the Glory of Our Nation* (London: Mercurius Britannicus, 1626)
Anon., *The voyage of the wandring knight shewing the whole course of mans life, how apt hee is to follow vanitie, and how hard it is for him to attaine to vertue* (London: William Stansby, 1626)
Dekker, Thomas, *The guls horne-booke* (London: Nicholas Okes] for R. S[ergier?], 1609)
Nicholls, Philip, *Sir Francis Drake revived calling upon this dull or effeminate age, to folowe his noble steps for golde & silver* (London: Edward Allde for Nicholas Bourne, 1626)
A proclamation commanding all inhabitants on the sea-coastes, or any ports or sea-townes, to make their speedy repaire unto, and continue at the places of their habitations there, during these times of danger (London: Bonham Norton and John Bill, 1626)
Purchas, Samuel, *Hakluytus Posthumus or Purchas his pilgrimes. Contayning a history of the world, in sea voyages & lande-travells, by Englishmen & others* (London: W[illiam] Stansby for H. Fetherstone, 1625)
Shirley, James, *The grateful servant a comedy* (London: B[ernard] A[lsop] and T[homas] F[awcet] for John Grove, 1630)

LATER WORKS

Primary sources
Calendar of State Papers Domestic: Charles I, 1625–1626 (London, 1858)
Calendar of State Papers (Venetian): 1623–1625 (London, 1912)
Calendar of State Papers (Venetian): 1625–1626 (London, 1913)
Early English Books Online, http://eebo.chadwyck.com/home
English Short Title Catalogue, http://estc.bl.uk
Greg, W. W., *A Bibliography of the English Printed Drama to the Restoration*, 4 vols (London: Oxford University Press, 1951)

152

FURTHER READING

Secondary sources

Bald, R. C., 'Review: Dick of Devonshire', *The Review of English Studies*, 8 (1957), 289

Bawcutt, N. W., 'New Revels Documents of Sir George Buc and Sir Henry Herbert, 1619–1662', *The Review of English Studies*, 35 (1984), 316–31

Bawcutt, N. W., ed., *The Control and Censorship of Caroline Drama: The Records of Sir Henry Herbert, Master of the Revels 1623–73* (Oxford: Oxford University Press, 1996)

Bellany, Alastair, 'Railing Rhymes Revisited: Libels, Scandals, and Early Stuart Politics', *History Compass*, 5 (2007), 1136–79

Boas, F. S., *The Diary of Thomas Crosfield* (Oxford: Oxford University Press, 1935)

Mrs Bray, *Traditions, Legends, Superstitions and Sketches of Devonshire on the Borders of the Tamar and the Tavy*, vol. 3 (London: John Murray, 1879)

Brooking Rowe, J., ed., *Richard Peeke of Tavistock: His Three to One, the Commendatory Verses and the Play of Dick of Devonshire* (Exeter: James G. Commin, 1905)

Cogswell, Thomas, 'The Politics of Propaganda: Charles I and the People in the 1620s', *The Journal of British Studies*, 29 (1990), 187–215

Dutton, Richard, *Licensing, Censorship and Authorship in Early Modern England* (Basingstoke: Palgrave, 2000)

Dutton, Richard, *Mastering the Revels: The Regulation and Censorship of Early Modern Drama* (Oxford: Oxford University Press, 2022)

Hirschfeld, Heather, *Joint Enterprises: Collaborative Drama and the Institutionalization of the English Renaissance Theatre* (Amherst: University of Massachusetts Press, 2004)

Ioppolo, Grace, *Dramatists and Their Manuscripts in the Age of Shakespeare, Jonson, Middleton and Heywood: Authorship, Authority and the Playhouse* (Abingdon: Routledge, 2006)

Kermode, Lloyd Edward, *Aliens and Englishness in Elizabethan Drama* (Cambridge: Cambridge University Press, 2009)

Lezra, Jacques, '"A Spaniard is no Englishman": The Ghost of Spain and the British Imaginary', *Journal of Medieval and Early Modern Studies*, 39 (2009), 119–41

Lost Plays Database, ed. Roslyn L. Knutson, David McInnis, Matthew Steggle, and Misha Teramura, http://www.lostplays.org (accessed 20 March 2023)

Love, Harold, *Scribal Publication in Seventeenth-Century England* (Oxford: Oxford University Press, 1993)

Marotti, Arthur F., and Bristol, Michael D., *Print, Manuscript and Performance: The Changing Relations of the Media in Early Modern England* (Columbus: Ohio State University Press, 2000)

Van den Berg, Sara, 'Marking His Place: Ben Jonson's Punctuation', *Early Modern Literary Studies*, 1 (1995), 1–25

Woudhuysen, Henry, *Sir Philip Sidney and the Circulation of Manuscripts 1558–1640* (Oxford: Clarendon Press, 1996)

Wright, George T., *Shakespeare's Metrical Art* (Berkeley: University of California Press, 1988)

Index

Algiers 7
Antonio and Mellida 18

Beeston, Christopher 15, 19
Blackfriars (playhouse) 18
Buckingham, Duke of 6, 24, 25, 26, 151

Cadiz 3, 4, 6, 7, 9, 12, 17, 24, 25, 26, 36, 38, 41, 42, 43, 44, 151
Cartwright the Younger, William 15, 17, 18, 19
Cecil, Edward 4, 17, 25, 26
Chapman, George 14, 118
  May Day 14
Charles I 9, 24, 25, 73
Cockpit (playhouse) 18–9
Craig, Hugh 2

Davenport, Robert 1
Dekker, Thomas 20, 35, 48, 95, 116
  Match Me In London 20
Drake, Sir Francis 1, 25, 28, 46, 47, 62, 77, 150
Dulwich College 15, 18
Dumb Knight, The 18
Dutch Provinces 26

Egerton 1994 1, 3, 13, 15–9, 30, 105, 108

Ford, John 1
France 8, 12, 38, 39, 67, 144, 151

Glanville, Sir John 4, 8, 26, 27, 36, 80, 137

Hawkins, Sir John 25, 150
Henslowe, Philip 19
Herbert, Henry 16, 20
Heywood, Thomas 1–4, 9, 10, 12, 13, 15, 18–21, 23, 27–30

Captives, The 18, 27
Dick of Devonshire 1–4, 7–10, 12–21, 23–4, 27, 31.
English Traveller, The 12–3
Late Lancashire Witches, The 10
Woman Killed With Kindness, A 10, 19

James I 7, 24, 25
Jonson, Ben 23
  Epicoene 23

King of Bohemia's Men 18
King's Company 18
King's Men 18

Lady Elizabeth's Players 18
Lisbon 7, 8, 111, 140, 149

Mead, Rev. 6, 7, 151
Meddus, Dr. 6, 25, 151
Merchant of Venice, The 22
Middleton, Thomas 14, 27, 35, 64, 68, 82, 94, 95, 129
  Blurt Master Constable 14, 48
  Game at Chess, A 14, 20, 27, 68, 82, 94, 129

Office of the Revels 3, 16
Olivares, Conde d' 6, 151

Paul's (playhouse) 18
Peeke, Richard 3, 4, 5, 6–13, 17, 27–9, 31, 59, 62, 131, 132, 145–8, 149
Plymouth 28, 29, 111
Prince Charles's Players 18
Purchas, Samuel 24

Queen Anne's Players of the Revels 18

154

INDEX

155

Queen Henrietta Maria's Men 15,
  18–9, 73
Queen of Bohemia's Men 18

Salisbury Court 18
Shirley, James 1, 21
  Grateful Servant, The 21
Spain 8, 11, 17, 21, 24, 25, 28, 30,
  39, 40, 44, 45, 46, 90, 131, 140,
  143, 144, 147, 151

Stationers' Register 3, 4
Stuteville, Sir Martin 7

Tavistock 9, 44, 62, 80, 131–2, 138,
  145, 148, 151

Whitefriars (playhouse) 18

EU authorised representative for GPSR:
Easy Access System Europe, Mustamäe tee 50,
10621 Tallinn, Estonia
gpsr.requests@easproject.com

www.ingramcontent.com/pod-product-compliance
Lightning Source LLC
LaVergne TN
LVHW050045200525
811683LV00004B/21